As always, Stephanie's words are a balm to overwhelmed women everywhere—each trying her hardest to live her life well. Throughout this beautiful book, Stephanie comes alongside you with the friendly tone of a dear friend and the wise teachings of a trusted mentor. *Create a Life You Love* delivers clarity, purpose, and the much-needed reminder that we are never alone.

Emily Ley, bestselling author, *Grace, Not Perfection*

Life is hard work. It comes with a lot of big questions and difficult decisions that will affect the rest of our lives. We can often feel so paralyzed by the pressure of hoping to do life "the right way" that we can forget to enjoy it. In *Create a Life You Love*, Stephanie May Wilson shares her personal experiences and knowledge she's learned over the years to remind us that it's important to be good stewards of the things we are given and that it's possible to love the lives we build along the way. This book was encouraging to me that even in hard, crazy, or unclear seasons I can live in faith and joy, creating a life I'm proud of.

Madison Prewett Troutt, speaker; TV personality;
bestselling author, *The Love Everybody Wants*

Stephanie leads the way with wisdom and experience, and this book is her showing you the heart she's wearing on her sleeve. Not only is she bound to become one of your favorite humans, but Stephanie is also the perfect guide to stand alongside you as you boldly build a life of beauty and intention. If you're at a crossroads where you're wanting something more or you're simply tired of living for the approval of other people—brew a cup of coffee and pick up this book!

Hannah Brencher, author, *Fighting Forward*,
Come Matter Here, and *The Unplugged Hours*

Create a Life You Love is your personal guide to crafting a life filled with purpose and joy. Stephanie is your guide to help you find your path, make meaningful choices, and enjoy the journey. I love this book!

Alli Worthington, entrepreneur; author,
Remaining You While Raising Them

Stephanie has long been one of my favorite writers. She just has a way of making you feel like you're chatting with your BFF at a long overdue girls' night. And in this book, she serves as equal parts best friend who gets it and mentor who's been there. She gently guides you as you learn to silence all the voices that may be overwhelming you through some of the most important decisions of your one precious life. This is a must-read!

Jordan Lee Dooley, two-time national
bestselling author; host, *SHE* podcast

Poignant, relatable, and oh-so-important, this book is a must-read for anyone on a journey to better themselves in a practical, applicable, and reasonable way. Stephanie is tuned in to real-life challenges, and her roadmap also accounts for the inevitable pitfalls and roadblocks, proving her understanding of the human experience and how each of our paths are unique. Add this book to your nightstand and you won't be disappointed.

Jasmine Roth, host, HGTV

Create a Life You Love is more than just a book; it's a life-changing journey, answering the big question, "What do I want to do with my life?" Easy to read and like having a wise friend by your side, it's perfect for those navigating the uncertainties of their twenties and thirties. Whether about moving, career choices, marriage, or motherhood, the author provides a ton of advice, clarity, and wisdom. Let this book be your guide to making those big decisions with confidence and joy!

Sazan Hendrix, author; content creator; podcaster

Stephanie leads with honesty, transparency, and authenticity. Her ability to understand the impact and navigate the weight of life's big decisions is unmatched. This book is yet another beacon of guidance for those who are tired of trying to figure out life all on their own. Full of encouragement and like talking to a good friend, Stephanie will guide you with wisdom and grace in *Create a Life You Love*.

Robin Long, founder/CEO, Lindywell; author, *Well to the Core*

Reading this book feels like talking to a big sister—not one who pretends to have it all figured out, but one who's willing to do life alongside you while reminding you that you're not alone during seasons of wondering and uncertainty. Stephanie makes creating a life you love feel not just attainable, but enjoyable, freeing, and empowering. When you pick this book up, you'll learn how to lay some heavy burdens down.

Danielle Coke Balfour, illustrator and author of *A Heart on Fire: 100 Meditations on Loving Your Neighbors Well*

Stephanie writes like she is your new best friend, and honestly, reading this book, you will feel like she is. She makes women feel seen, meets them where they are, and then delivers practical tools to help them find freedom from societal pressures and comparison to create a life they *love*. I love this book, and I hope every single woman (pun intended) picks it up.

Kait Tomlin, national bestselling author; dating coach, founder, Heart of Dating

Create a Life You Love is a welcome invitation to build life on your own terms. Wilson walks you through thoughtful insights to take agency in your own life.

Eve Rodsky, author, *Fair Play*

If you want to create a life you'll love—and create a life with love in it—then join Stephanie May Wilson as she takes on "The Woman Question" and more. You'll be glad you did.

Meg Jay, PhD, author, *The Twentysomething Treatment* and *The Defining Decade*

CREATE
A LIFE
YOU LOVE

ALSO BY
STEPHANIE MAY WILSON

CREATE

A LIFE

YOU LOVE

HOW TO QUIET OUTSIDE VOICES
SO YOU CAN FINALLY HEAR YOUR OWN

STEPHANIE MAY WILSON

ZONDERVAN
BOOKS

To my mom, Dr. Nancy Mayfield—
You showed me that it's possible
to be a great mom and have a career
you love. Thank you for being in my
corner as I work to do the same.

To my daughters, Annie and Quinn—
May you each create a life you love. I'll be right
here, cheering you on every step of the way.

CONTENTS

INTRODUCTION

Have you seen these? These shoes would be just perfect."
The bridal shop saleswoman held up a pair of glittery, blueish ballet flats that looked eerily similar to the shoes I'd worn to my freshman homecoming dance.

They fit the bill, I guess. I was getting married in a garden, so I definitely needed to wear flats. And I suppose the glitter made them somewhat formal, which was good for a black-tie wedding.

But I wasn't sure they were what I really wanted.

"Honestly, I think I'd just be happy wearing some plain sandals," I told her. "My dress is so long, you'll never see my feet. I just want to be comfortable, and I'm spending so much money on other things, this just isn't a high priority for me!"

"You can't get married in sandals," the saleswoman admonished. "No, no, these are perfect," she said as she pressed the shoes into my hands. "These are the ones. I'm sure of it."

I was glad she was sure, because I certainly wasn't. I *was* sure that I was ready to get out of there, though.

My mom and I had been shopping for hours, and I'd been wedding planning for months. I was hungry and tired and sick of making decisions, so even though these shoes looked nothing like me and didn't fit the way I wanted to look and feel on my wedding day, I took them to the counter, and $175 later, they were mine. "It's fine," I told myself. "I'll get used to them. They'll be fine."

But I didn't get used to them. In fact, every time I saw them—taunting me from the corner of my bedroom—I disliked them even more. I was mad at those shoes, and even more, I was mad at myself. I was mad that I didn't speak up for myself, mad that I let her talk me into something I didn't want, mad that I let a stranger have so much influence over such an important day in my life. And the fact that the dumb shoes were so expensive made me feel even worse.

A few days later, still mad, I called my best friend. "I should just keep them, shouldn't I? The saleslady said it was weird to get married in sandals, and she's right. Right? I need to just get over it. It's not like anyone will see them anyway."

"No!" she said. "Stephanie, this is your wedding day. It should look and feel like *you*. Who cares what this random stranger thinks is weird? If you want to get married in sandals, do it."

She was right, and so I did.

I returned the awful wedding shoes, spent that money instead on a gorgeous hand-stitched sash to go around my dress, and bought a pair of simple gold sandals. I felt beautiful on my wedding day, and my feet didn't hurt one bit. No regrets.

I wish I could say the same for every other major life decision I've made. I wish I could say that I never again let someone else's vision for my life overpower my own. But I've done it again—more than once—and I'm sure you have too. Because if you're anything like me, it can be hard to hear your own voice, let alone trust it and follow where it leads. Or maybe part of you balks at the idea that you can (and even should!) get what you want in life.

We're so used to hearing statements like "Life is hard," "Life's not fair," and "That's just how it is," that it can feel silly and unrealistic to think it's even possible to create a life you love, let alone that it's something you should spend time striving to achieve. We don't want to be spoiled or entitled or naive, thinking life will always be fun and easy or expecting to get everything we want.

But that's not what we're talking about here, because that's not actually what you're looking for, is it?

You're not looking for a perfect life, but you are looking for a great one. You know that the best, most important things in life require grit and perseverance and courage—and you're up for the challenge (on most days, that is!). You are smart and resilient. You do hard things. You're not looking for a magic pill or an instant fix, but you might need some help moving forward, because sometimes you feel stuck or lost—or maybe both.

Maybe you're about to have a big birthday and you're not where you thought you'd be by this point in your life. Maybe you're making a massive decision—you're swimming in lists of pros and cons and still don't know what to do. Maybe you know *exactly* what you want in life but you don't know how to get it, or maybe you have no clue what you want, but you know you don't want what you're "supposed to want" and the conflict raging inside you as a result is positively consuming.

I've walked hundreds of thousands of women through some of the biggest decisions of their lives, so I know that when you're in the middle of a major turning point, every decision feels critical. Your life feels like a carefully built but teetering tower, and you're afraid that if you breathe wrong—or, heaven forbid, sneeze—you're going to send all the pieces crashing to the ground and ruin your life forever. But even more than being afraid you're going to get it wrong, you just really want to get it right.

You know you get one life, one shot, and you don't want to waste it! You want to build a life that's fulfilling, a life you're proud of, a life you're excited to wake up to every day (or at least most days!). You want to make the most of your life—in big, sweeping, world-changing ways, but also in the small, day-to-day, "this is too good to miss" moments.

You want to create a life you love—and that's a good thing.

Friend, it's not silly or entitled or unrealistic to want to love your life. It's a beautiful thing to pursue a life of meaning and joy—and it's something within reach.

Life is too short to wear shoes that don't fit—whether your feet, your style, or your life—especially when there are seven hundred gazillion other options to choose from. It's not selfish to want to find shoes that fit—in fact, it's silly not to. The same is true about life.

In some areas of life, you get extra points for "sucking it up"—for accepting a difficult situation and making the most of it. So you push through, you endure, you stick it out, you finish the race, and you're better for it. But that's not always the case. Good things aren't always hard, and hard things aren't always good. Not every difficult and uncomfortable path has a prize at the end of it. There's simply no prize for getting married in shoes you hate. Similarly, there's no prize for dedicating your time and energy to building a life you don't actually want to live—and thereby missing out on the life you really do want.

You don't always get to choose your circumstances, of course, and we all have day-to-day responsibilities we can't neglect. But almost always, we have choices available to us that would help our lives fit us a little bit better. That's what this book is about. It's about being a good steward of the gift that is your life, about doing what you can with what you've been given. You can't control every element of your life, but there is so much you *can* do—and your life will be so much better if you participate in creating it.

Let's be honest—creating a life you love can be hard. But that's why I'm here to help.

Through my podcast, books, and online courses, I've become a go-to guide for women in their twenties and thirties as they navigate this life season's biggest decisions and transitions—being single and navigating relationships, getting engaged and then married, pursuing a career, moving to a new city, and (this is the enormous transition I've been going through lately!) becoming a mom.

I'm on a mission to be the person I needed when I was younger: a guide, a sounding board, and a friend who's both been where you are and gotten to where you want to go. I've walked hundreds of thousands of women through the most high-stakes, high-pressure era of their lives, and I'm here to help you too.

Before we get started, I want to make you a few promises.

First, I promise that this is a safe place. I want to say this right up front, because making the biggest decisions of your life is—surprise, surprise—really hard. This isn't a place where you have to pretend you have it all together. This isn't a networking event, a class reunion, a first date, or a job interview. You don't have to have a polished, impressive answer to the question "So, what are you going to do next?"—and you're not going to get a single side-eye if your answer is "Honestly, I have no idea."

That brings us to my second promise: I promise I will not be yet another voice telling you what to do.

This isn't a book about how I built a life I love and how you can build one just like it. This is a safe place to put some pieces of your own life together—not *my* way, but *your* way.

Many of the people in your life will have opinions about the decisions you make. That's because they're part of your life. They have a horse in the race. Maybe they're the ones who footed the bill for the degree you may or may not end up using, or maybe all their hopes and dreams for grandkids rest uncomfortably on your reproductive system. Or maybe their finances and future descendants aren't quite so closely tied to your life choices, but they do love you and want the best for you—so they make sure to weigh in. The problem is, most people's definition of "best" sounds an awful lot like the decisions they made (or didn't make but wish they had) in their own lives. It's great to have an engaged support system, but it gets tricky when your support system has a clearer vision for your life than you do.

I don't have a specific vision for your life. I care about you, and I care how your life turns out, but I don't care what you decide to do. I want your life to turn out the way *you* want it to. So in this book we're going to turn down the volume on the people telling you what to do and how you should do it. And we're going to make space for you to get quiet enough to listen to your own hopes and dreams—to finally hear what you need and want.

You can decide to paint your hair, your face, and every room in your house bright blue, or you can live in a nudist colony (are those really a thing?) and spend the rest of your days as free as can be. You can be a florist in Frankfurt or a ventriloquist in Venezuela, or you can live in a high-rise in New York, have four different cell phones, and constantly yell into them "Buy, buy, buy! No, sell, sell, sell!" like they do in the movies. You can join the military or a monastery. You can have twelve kids or no kids. You can get married, you can be single, you can be a serial dater, or you can be in a long-term, committed relationship but never walk down the aisle.

I don't care *what* you choose. I just care that *you* choose.

My prayer is that when you finish this book, you will feel both empowered and equipped to make intentional decisions about your life—so that you can live a life you're proud of and excited about, a life that looks and feels like *you*.

Get comfy and get excited, friend. There are so many good things ahead.

All my love,

PART ONE

WHY DOES

IT FEEL

SO HARD?

CHAPTER ONE

THE UNNAMED DECADE WHERE IT ALL GETS DECIDED

I knew this would happen. I absolutely, positively knew this would happen.

I told my mom. I called it months before. It's the reason I requested, as she was putting together her famously elaborate Thanksgiving table, that she seat me next to literally anybody *but* my Aunt Sharon.

I knew what Aunt Sharon would ask, and I knew it would bother me (even though I wished it wouldn't). I didn't want to spend yet another family dinner feeling that way.

But here I was anyway, my turkey-shaped place card sitting right next to, yep, my Aunt Sharon's. Mom must have forgotten. And of course Aunt Sharon took her seat before I had a chance to make the switch.

I love my Aunt Sharon, and I know my Aunt Sharon loves me. But that doesn't keep her from accidentally stomping on an emotional land mine every time I see her.[*]

---

[*] Note: The potential subject matter for this common familial interaction may include, but is not limited to: college applications; selection of majors and minors; postgrad plans; job transitions; home purchases; dating; engagements; wedding plans; fertility; timing of first, second, and all subsequent children; breastfeeding; and childcare—just to name a few. I've had to answer questions that were both pointed and public about all these topics, and I know I'm not the only one.

It happened early that year. The spotlight reached me before the basket of rolls did.

Aunt Sharon turned to me and in a much-too-loud voice asked, *"So, are you seeing anyone special?"*

Yep, there it was. The question I'd been dreading for the last several months. I knew it was coming, but that didn't make it sting any less.

The answer to her question was no. I was not seeing anyone special. I wished I was seeing someone special. But so far, my love life had been a long string of almosts, not-quites, and not-even-closes.

But Aunt Sharon wasn't finished. This year, she tacked on a comment I didn't see coming:

"You know, you're not getting any younger. I was married with three kids by the time I was your age."

And there it was: one of the worst things you can say to a woman.

My cheeks flushed hot. I was equal parts embarrassed and angry, and I willed myself not to cry.

My aunt's question and follow-up comment probably seemed innocent enough to my extended family seated around the table (who had all paused their own conversations to hear my answer). Aunt Sharon wasn't trying to hurt my feelings. She was making conversation, taking an interest in my life. She cared about me.

The problem was that her words reinforced the fear that was genuinely keeping me up at night—the fear I spent most of my time trying to talk myself out of. I was afraid that my dreams for my life might never come true. I wasn't where I wanted to be in life, I had no idea how to move forward, and I was afraid I was running out of time.

The Decade-ish of Decisions

Welcome to the decade-ish where your whole life gets decided. It's this weird, wonderful, and wildly difficult span of years somewhere between the ages of twenty-five and forty-ish, during which you'll make the most biographically significant decisions of your life—all at the same time.

Who you are, what you want to do with your life, where you'll call home, who your people are, which person you'll share your life with, and whether you'll have kids—the major plot points of your life are often decided within just a few short years. The stakes are high. The things you do (and don't do!) during this time can have ripple effects across years and even generations, and you do *not* want to look back and have regrets.

Everyone's experience is different, certainly, but looking back, it feels like the pressure to figure out what I wanted to do with my life really cranked up around my twenty-fifth birthday. Sure, I'd made some significant life decisions before turning twenty-five, but it always felt like there was a little more grace around the edges—like bowling with bumpers.

Some of us graduate college and step straight onto a prescribed path. We know exactly what's expected of us and when. (Whether or not we feel like we can meet those expectations is another story entirely.) But for many of us, our early twenties feel a bit like we've fallen off the edge of the map. We've completed the assignment. We got the degree. We've followed a specific set of instructions for twenty-two whole years and then . . . what comes next? Our futures are suddenly limitless—and also, totally our responsibility.

Thankfully, society seems to view our early twenties as one long grace period. Everyone is wandering around, trying, failing, asking big questions, and taking their time figuring out the answers. Our early twenties are the time to backpack the world, move across the country for jobs that pay nothing, and pursue wild dreams. (That's what I did, anyway).

Everyone's trying things out and seeing what works. It's like an Italian cooking class. There's a little too much wine and there's pasta everywhere, and everyone is flinging spaghetti at the wall and seeing what sticks.

But overnight, all of that seems to change.

You wake up one day and it seems like everyone suddenly knows who they are and where they're going in life. And the second you see one person making big decisions and moving forward, it feels like you should be too. The bumpers are gone. This is your real, actual life—and you have to figure it out, and fast! One day you feel like you have all the time in the world; the next, you're behind, and as you see more and more people getting engaged, or buying houses, or getting "real jobs," or having babies, you feel like you might be running out of time. It feels like the margin of error is thin, and you *really* don't want to screw this up.

Do I Stay or Do I Go?

The first major fork in the road I faced during these years was a common dilemma: do I stay or do I go?

I was interning with my church's college group (having recently abandoned my brand-new journalism degree—sorry, Mom and Dad!), as a small group leader and mentor to a group of twenty-seven sorority girls. I loved the work so much, I was pretty sure I'd found the thing I wanted to do for the rest of my life. I wanted to be a pastor.

But then, in an instant, everything changed. I was having dinner with my friend Jacy when she mentioned a trip she'd heard about. It was a yearlong humanitarian trip where the participants lived out of backpacks and volunteered with different nonprofit organizations in eastern Europe, eastern Africa, and southeast Asia.

She mentioned it in passing, barely noticing that she'd planted a little seed. But by the time I got in my car and was driving home, that seed had grown into a forest. I had to know more about this trip.

The backpack thing felt like a bit of a stretch for me, but the traveling was right up my alley. I'd *always* wanted to do something like this. I couldn't believe it might actually be an option.

I did a ton of research, filled out the application, did an interview, and just two weeks later got accepted. The spot was mine if I wanted it. Did I want it? Now I had to decide.

The decision might sound like a no-brainer. Did I want to travel around the world for a year? Uh, yes. Yes, I did. But like most decisions, it wasn't that simple.

If I did this trip, I'd be leaving behind my home, my family, my friends, and every bit of my comfort zone—just to name a few minor things. Doing the trip would mean leaving my current job, which also meant giving up future opportunities I'd been working for all year. It would mean a delay in my career, or potentially even a setback.

But none of those things were my biggest concern. My real worry was that I'd always thought I'd get married in my mid-twenties, and I was *sure* I'd meet my person in my home state of Colorado. If I left home at this stage in my life, I worried I'd be putting an important dream for my life on hold, if not giving it up altogether.

Now, maybe my worries sound dramatic. The trip was just one year, right? But it was bigger than that. I knew this would be a life-changing experience, that I would almost certainly come home different (if I decided to come home at all!). But did I *want* my life to change? Did I want to be different? It felt like I was choosing a trajectory—making a choice that would set off a domino effect in one direction or another. I had to choose between Door A and Door B—and I had to make my choice without knowing where either of them would lead.

I lay awake night after night, staring up at my ceiling—willing it to tell me what to do. I felt unqualified to make such a big decision. Who gave me the authority to determine the direction of my life, anyway? It felt like just ten minutes ago I was a college student sledding down snowbanks on cafeteria trays. Shouldn't I have to pass some sort of prep course before the reins of my life are just handed over to me? Is anyone going to check my work here?

I'm sure you've been kept up at night by decisions like this too.

Maybe you're trying to decide between two possibilities. Do you take Job A or Job B? Do you move to this city or back to that one? Is he the one or should you keep looking? Are you ready to have a baby? These are the kinds of decisions that can change everything.

Maybe you know *exactly* what you want, you just have no idea how to get it. Maybe you have a dream that—despite your best efforts—stays just out of reach, leaving you afraid that it may never come true.

Maybe some pieces of your life have come together beautifully, but in other areas you have major gaps you can't seem to fill. You're married to a great guy, but you feel lost when it comes to work. Or you're established and growing in a career you love, but your love life feels like a desert wasteland.

Or maybe you're juggling several dreams and aren't sure how to fit them together. Maybe you have big career ambitions but also want to have kids someday, and you're trying to figure out the timing (and the math) of how to do both. "If I get married by age _____, then I'll only have ____ years before I need to start trying to get pregnant. But I need to get to this place in my career before all of that. . . ." You're trying to cram so much into what feels like so little time. You're wondering, "Will I have to quit my job to raise kids? Can I afford childcare on my current salary? If I keep working, will I ever see my kids? Will one of my dreams cost me the other?"

Not only are you facing massive decisions, playing Tetris with your hopes and dreams, your body, your finances, and your most important relationships, but it also feels like the whole world is leaning over your shoulder, telling you what to do.

Cue the Backseat Drivers

These big life decisions are especially difficult because they're so public. Your friends and family can seem like paparazzi keeping their eagle eyes trained on your left ring finger, your drink order, and your belly. (*"She's not drinking! Do you think she's pregnant? Is that a bump?"*)

Because this season of life is so significant, you may find yourself with a lot of spectators, critics, backseat drivers, and couch-cushion coaches. People will have opinions about what you do, why you do it, and how you do it, and it's made even harder by people like Aunt Sharon who aren't trying to be cruel but who frequently ask for updates about your life and seem disappointed by or critical of whatever you tell them.

For better or worse, we don't show up to our life's biggest turning points empty-handed. We're flanked by pressure, comparison, opinions, and expectations—both ours and other people's.

There will be people who pry into your life, asking pointed questions, totally undeterred by your polite attempts to change the subject. They're the unsolicited advice givers, the kings and queens of the side-eye, the ones who like to start sentences by saying, "You know, when I was your age . . ."

But their input doesn't help, because they don't have all the information. Their advice only reinforces your worry that maybe the problem isn't the problem—*you* are. And if you were smarter, stronger, or better—or just tried harder—this would be easier.

These people also tend to take great offense when you make a decision that's different from the one they made, because it makes them feel like you're implying they did it wrong. They want you to validate their decisions by making the same ones they did, and if you don't, they'll find a passive-aggressive way to let you know they're not pleased.

"Oh, *wow*, what an *interesting* choice."

This is all made even worse by our society's *still* often narrow view of what it looks like to be a successful woman of a certain age. If you're not married and don't have kids, you're sometimes treated as less-than, stuck at society's kids' table, instead of as a card-carrying adult.

The worst offender when it comes to this kind of treatment might just be church, especially if you're single. Most churches don't know what to do with single women. Either they have no groups, resources, or chances to connect with other people who are single and don't have kids, or they have a half-hearted "singles ministry" that ends up being an awkward mix of people of all ages who have nothing in common other than their lack of a wedding ring.

The pressure hits an all-time high for women in our thirties. Turning thirty can feel like a border crossing—like you have to stop for inspection, and a tough-looking guard with a handlebar mustache asks to see your adulthood credentials. If your life doesn't look a certain way by this point, there's definitely something wrong with you—or at least that's what it feels like.

If this is hitting home, know that you're not alone. I've been there. I've been through all of this, and I've been through it recently. I'm not in the thick of it anymore, but I still have mud on my shoes from walking this path. My journey involved a *lot* of trial and error along the way. But do you know what? I love how it turned out.

I'm walking out of this decade-ish having genuinely enjoyed these years. I worked hard to identify what's important to me and I've tried to build my life accordingly. I'm walking out of these years having built a marriage, a family, a community, a career, a home, and a life. Piece by piece, decision by decision, I've created a life I'm excited about, a life I'm proud of, a life I truly love.

Knowing how hard but also formative these years are, I've made it my mission to help other women create lives they love too.

As I went through the major decisions and transitions these years held, and as I've heard countless other women expressing the same fears and frustrations I'd experienced, I started to wonder, "What is happening here?" I wanted to understand more about this time in women's lives, why it's so dang hard, and how we can make it easier.

And that's when I started to do some digging.

What I found blew me away. I felt like I'd gone to pick up an ice cube and ended up with an iceberg. There was so much lurking below the surface. It turns out what I went through during these years—and what you might be going through right now—this isn't a me problem, this isn't a you problem, this is an *us* problem (*gestures to all women everywhere for all of time*). Here's what I discovered . . .

CHAPTER TWO

THIS IS *NOT* ALL IN YOUR HEAD

The decisions you're trying to navigate right now, the season you're walking through—it feels like a lot because it *is* a lot. This is not all in your head. You're not the only one finding this season of life to be hard. You're not crazy, and you're not making this up.

While a lot of the pressure of this season is unfounded, unfair, and wildly unhelpful (you are *not* less-than if you're not married and a mom by a certain birthday!), the stakes for this time in our lives are legitimately high.

These are foundational years. It's the time when we build our identities, our careers, our homes, and our families—and it's all happening at the exact same time.

Research has shown that 80 percent of our life's most defining moments happen before our thirty-fifth birthday.[1] And we feel that, don't we?

The average college student graduates at twenty-two. You have a newly minted degree that may or may not actually be useful, and you're off to the races. You have a little bit of wiggle room to try out some different paths during those first few years, but the pressure soon starts to build. You've heard that your lifetime earning potential is largely determined by what you do in the first ten years of your career, so you want to take these years seriously.

Add to the unhelpful career pressure the fact that this is also the best time to save for retirement. Your future self will thank you a million times over if you have the foresight to invest some money early. But you likely aren't thinking about how you're going to get through retirement—you're too busy thinking about how you're going to get through this week. (Also, who has extra money right now? Anybody?)

And you're trying to make all these decisions before your brain has fully developed. Cool, right? According to the National Institute of Mental Health, "The brain finishes developing and maturing in the mid-to-late twenties. The part of the brain behind the forehead, called the prefrontal cortex, is one of the last parts to mature. This area is responsible for skills like planning, prioritizing, and making good decisions."[2] Cool, cool, cool. It feels like we're flying blind because we pretty much are.

Not only are our brains still changing during this time, but our personalities are too. Research shows that our personalities change more during our twenties than any time before or after.[3] This is truly our life's primary season of self-discovery.

Add to all of this the crushing pressure (both external and internal) to meet and marry your person during these years, and it's no wonder we feel anxious.

Now, let's say you're on a roll and you have some elements of your life exactly how you want them. You've narrowed down your field of interest in your career, you have some great friends, and maybe you're even in a semi-serious relationship with real potential. Amazing!

But wait, here comes another wrench. Just as you're starting to gain some traction—figuring out who you are and what you want to do, getting the hang of the relationship thing, and building momentum in your career—your biological clock shows up.

Biological Clock: *Knocks on office door* *Hey, excuse me, you weren't busy, were you?* (Doesn't pause for a response, comes on in, sits down and props feet up on your desk.) *Just wanted to give you a heads up that if you want to have children, you're going to need to do it . . . like . . .* *checks watch* *now.*

Great, just great. As if you needed any more pressure, now your body's going to turn on you too? How is it possible that our reproductive systems and our minds and hearts could be on such different pages when it comes to our life plans? But for a lot of us, they are. Our peak reproductive years are already over by the time many of us feel like we're ready to become parents.

It's all just too much. So if you feel like you're losing your mind as you try to figure out what you want to do with your life, you're not alone. These years can feel like you're sitting at a table with a thousand-piece puzzle spread out in front of you, and you have to figure out how all the pieces fit together while a too-loud clock ticks beside you and a bunch of people lean over your shoulder telling you what to do.

And of course, external pressures aren't the only ones we're dealing with. We also have our own expectations and dreams for ourselves and our lives, as well as the ideas we've internalized about what we're "supposed" to do. And all the while there's the infuriating reality of our biological clocks, which seem to tick faster and louder with each passing day.

We're facing change after change, transition after transition, gigantic life decision after gigantic life decision, with hardly a moment in between to catch our breaths. And these changes rarely have the decency to happen one right after another. The biggest, trickiest, most confusing, and most defining moments of our lives instead have the audacity to overlap.

A dear friend of mine once called this the "cosmic double-booking" of this season—the most pivotal moments for our relationship decisions, our career, our self-discovery, and our ability to have children . . . the fact that they're all happening at the same time is just unforgivable. *Do you hear me, God, society, whoever's at fault here? Un. For. Give. Able.*

We Should Start a Club

The more I learned about this uniquely challenging season of life, the more shocked I became at what I could not find: a name for it. For the longest time, I didn't know what to call this time in our lives. I knew what it felt like, I knew what was so hard and overwhelming and frustrating about it—and I was hearing countless women share similar reflections as we talked over coffee and over email.

But for such an important time in women's lives, the decade-ish when we make many of the decisions that will come to define our lives, these years have somehow gone unnamed. They're not our twenties or our thirties. They're both, and yet the exact time frame is a little different for everybody. They're not our postgrad years, and while we are still young and we are adults, "young adult" feels patronizing. Researcher Jeffrey Jensen Arnett coined the term "emerging adulthood," but that only refers to people between the ages of eighteen to twenty-five.[4] And while many aspects of this season certainly look and feel and quack like a crisis—we're certainly asking the same questions: "What am I doing with my life? What's the rest of my life going to look like? What's the point of everything?"—we don't fit neatly into either quarter or midlife.

When something doesn't have a name, it's hard to talk about. When life feels overwhelming and our hard circumstances feel unique to us rather than being part of a defined experience everyone else travels through too, we're naturally going to feel alone. When we don't have a name for what we're going through, it's easy to feel like we might be crazy, like we're falling apart and we're the only ones.

When I was single, I dreaded the day my best friends would get married, and when I was married, I cried and cried the day my best friend told me she was pregnant. It's not that I wasn't happy for them. I was. But I was also terrified that they'd leave me behind. For the longest time, I bought into the fallacy that a woman loses her ability to relate to her single friends the second she walks down the aisle, and that women who have kids have nothing in common with women who don't. I thought that our lives had to look the same for us to travel through them together.

But that's just not how it works. Our circumstances may be different, but the questions we're asking, the hopes we're holding, and the fears we're wrestling during this time of life are all remarkably similar—and when we can recognize and gather around the truth that we're all in this together, we get to go through it together, which makes it all so much easier. It really does.

More and more studies are starting to back up the idea that life is better when we're in it together. A study from the University of Virginia had participants stand at the bottom of a hill, wearing heavy backpacks, and asked them to rate the steepness of the hill. Participants who had a friend standing next to them when they made their assessment consistently rated the hill less steep than did participants who stood alone. Having a friend nearby when we're facing an obstacle makes the obstacle feel more manageable.[5]

And having the support of a friend doesn't just make challenges feel less daunting, it actually changes how our brains react to stressful situations. In another University of Virginia study, researchers found that during a stressful situation, holding the hand of a loved one decreases the brain's stress reaction—reducing stress hormones like cortisol and adrenaline.[6]

And this really matters—not just in the moment, but for our long-term health and life expectancy. Studies since the 1980s have shown that if a person has no ties to friends, family, or community, their chance of dying early may be 50 percent higher than if they did. Or, put another way, social isolation increases a person's chance of early death more than smoking twenty cigarettes a day.[7] Yikes!

We can't walk through life alone, and we can't walk through these years alone either. We have to talk about what we're going through—connect over this season of life and recognize how much we're all up against. Otherwise we could accidentally find ourselves believing that we're weak for thinking this is hard, or believing that we're the only ones going through it.

This couldn't be further from the truth. You're not weak, and you're not alone. You're just living in what I've started calling our Everything Era—the decade-ish when it all gets decided—those pesky years between the ages of twenty-five and forty-ish when we're tasked with making the most biographically significant decisions of our lives, all at the same time. (We really should start a club, and we need matching t-shirts.)

But how did we get here? That was my next question as I started to unpack the enormity of this season of life. Have these years always been this hard for women? How has everyone before me figured this out?

It turns out, it's a long story.

CHAPTER THREE

IT'S A LONG STORY

The more I've learned about our history as women, the more clearly I see the obstacles we're facing today. So before we talk about the future, let's take a minute to look at the past.

It turns out that behind the stress and pressure of the "What am I supposed to do with my life?" question—as well as the specific questions we're all asking about career, marriage, motherhood, and more—well, there's some history there. And the history behind these questions helps explain how heavy and taxing and impossible it feels to answer them. The Everything Era is like an iceberg—what you see is big, and what's hiding under the surface is even bigger.

When it comes to the pressure and expectations and sheer number of backseat drivers leaning over our shoulders during this season of life—that's not new and it's not imagined. The question of how women are to spend these years of their lives (specifically, their reproductive years) has been hotly debated (mostly by men) for centuries.

There's even a name for it, if you can believe it: The Woman Question.

I'm not kidding.

"The Woman Question" (originally posed in French as the "querelle des femmes") refers to a centuries-long debate about the nature of women. As far back as the 1400s, scholars, doctors, politicians, writers, church leaders (almost all men!), and society as a whole have all debated about women's rights and roles in society. The questions have included where women belong, what their place in society is, what they're capable of—and conversely, where women shouldn't be, what they shouldn't be allowed to do, and what they can't possibly be capable of.[1]

There are truly countless examples to choose from, but here's a particularly ridiculous (and insulting) one. In the late 1800s, there was a commonly held belief that the human body couldn't multitask. People believed that the body didn't have enough resources or energy to perform multiple functions at a time, so if a person's body was working hard to do one thing, it couldn't also be doing something else. As a result of this idea, there was a massive (and highly effective) push against women's admission to universities. Many concluded that higher education would divert too many resources up to a woman's brain, thereby causing her uterus to atrophy.[2]

There are no words.

The Woman Question hasn't gone anywhere. It's still being asked and answered today, and while a lot has changed since the 1400s, the voices with the most influence and decision-making power are still mostly male (think about Congress, the Supreme Court, church leaders, and more). They're asking The Woman Question, and truthfully, so are we: Where do I fit? What am I supposed to be doing? What contribution can I make in the world?

Men ask similar questions in this stage of life. They feel the weight of expectation, uncertainty, and insecurity too. But they don't have the same undercurrent yanking at their ankles that women do. Men have always been seen as the masters of their own destinies. It's only recently that women have had enough power and autonomy to ask, "What do I want to do with my life?" with more than a few set options to choose from.

Recognizing the pressures women have been under throughout history helps me feel like I'm not alone. I'm part of a large sisterhood, and I'm honored to be. This truth is especially helpful to me during times when I start to wonder if the pressure I'm feeling is imagined—if the expectations I'm sensing are really as heavy and forceful as they feel. As I look back at the centuries of pressure and expectations and opinions about women's lives and how they should spend them, I see that yes, this actually is as big as it feels. And that's so validating. It helps me be kinder to myself as I navigate all of this. I hope it helps you too.

The Opinions Have *Always* Been There. The Options Haven't.

Not only is it helpful for me to know that this pressure isn't new—that women have always had people breathing down their necks telling them what they should do and how they should live—but also, the more I find out about the expectations placed on women throughout history, the more I understand why some of the decisions I'm trying to make in my own life today feel so heavy.

So before we move on, we're going to do a quick women's history lesson. You with me? Even if you're not a history buff, this is important. As we look at what women have been expected to do throughout the years, I have a feeling that you'll start to spot the origin, the root, of some of the heaviest expectations you're carrying around today. I know I did.

For most of history, women have had next to no authority over their own lives. For centuries they were lumped into a similar category as children—provided for by the men who presided over them, but having little autonomy to make decisions for themselves or about their futures. (In the United States, many banks required women to have a male co-signer before they'd approve them for a credit card or a loan—a practice that wasn't outlawed until 1974!)[3]

Only a small percentage of women throughout history have had the privilege of wrestling with the question "What do I want to do with my life?" with any real options to choose from. Let's take a quick look at what those options have looked like throughout the years, shall we?

If we could zoom back through thousands of years of history, we'd see that in many societies and for many, many years, families lived as their own small, self-contained communities. They grew their own food and made their own clothing and built their own homes, and there wasn't a lot of interconnectedness between their well-being and that of other households—especially ones that were far away. If a family was struggling, it wasn't because of a turn in the market, but rather, a turn in the weather. And the social structure was patriarchal. Men were in charge at every level. At home, the father or eldest son was in charge, in church it was the male priest or minister, and at the larger community level were the "town fathers," the local nobility or, as they put it in Puritan society, "the nursing fathers of the Commonwealth."[4] (Of course, there have been a handful of matriarchal societies around the world too—but they're definitely the exception rather than the rule!)

Even though women didn't have authority within these patriarchal social structures, they did have a massive role to play. They were the Swiss Army knives of the family compound, the Jills of all trades. They were responsible for growing food, caring for animals, slaughtering animals, turning milk into cheese and butter, weaving fabric, and making clothing out of that fabric to keep everyone warm and dry. In addition, they were responsible for having babies, delivering babies, raising babies, teaching babies, and more and more and more. They were also the community doctors. Women were busy and they were important. Their depth and breadth of wisdom made them essential to the survival of their families.

But when the Industrial Revolution began in the latter half of the eighteenth century, everything changed.

Previously the whole family had needed to work the family farm, but now with machines and tools that could do the same jobs in half the time, there was opportunity for many of the family members to do something else. And this was perfect, because new factories were popping up every day, and these factories needed workers—and a lot of them. England, where the Industrial Revolution began, is a great example. In 1800 only 9 percent of the population lived in urban areas. By 1900, that number had risen to 62 percent.[5]

Daily life no longer revolved around the home. People no longer had to use their time and skills to create goods for their own family; instead, they could use their time and skills to work for someone else in exchange for money to buy those goods for the family. Many daily tasks moved to the cities, the factories, and the marketplace—and this begged the question of whether women should move with them. In this way, the Industrial Revolution brought up The Woman Question with even more urgency: now that the two were separate, was a woman's place at home or at work?

There were people arguing on both sides. Industry was booming, and some thought that everyone—men, women, and children—should direct their activities toward whatever would produce the most. But then there were the romantics, who, in the face of the harsh, dirty, and dangerous world of factories and the marketplace, wanted men's homes to be a soft place for them to land at the end of a long day. Romanticism won. Society firmly decided that a woman's place was in the home, and with that proclamation came a new set of requirements, a new definition for what it meant to be feminine and a "true woman." (This value system came to be known by historians as "The Cult of Domesticity" or "The Cult of True Womanhood.")

Under the Cult of Domesticity, "true women" were expected to uphold four virtues:

Piety: Religion was encouraged because, unlike intellectual pursuits, it wasn't thought to take women away from their proper sphere (their homes), and it was also beneficial for helping them keep their longings under control—which brings us to . . .

Purity: Purity was an essential tenet of the Cult of Domesticity. Virginity was considered a woman's prize possession—something that should be fiercely protected until her wedding night. And after a woman was married she was expected to keep her thoughts and actions pure, as well as remaining completely faithful to her husband.

Submission: Within the Cult of Domesticity, men were thought to be superior to women as part of God's design for the world. Therefore, women were expected to exhibit childlike submission and obedience to the men in their lives.

Domesticity: "True women" were supposed to remain in their homes, caring for their husbands and children. Women were thought to be too mentally and physically frail to leave home; suitable activities for women included domestic pursuits like housework, reading (but only religious biographies!), needlepoint, cooking, and tending flowers.[6]

Now, of course, this was the ideal, and it was only really achievable by white women with wealthy husbands. If you weren't married, wealthy, and white, you likely had to work outside the home in jobs that were often dangerous, dirty, and underpaid.[7] If you had children, you'd bring them with you, and as soon as they were big enough to be helpful, they'd work too. So, not every woman could strictly uphold the four virtues of the Cult of Domesticity, but even when you can't achieve an ideal, it doesn't let you off the hook from feeling like you're supposed to.

The Cult of Domesticity took a backseat with the start of World War II. Millions of young men were drafted to fight in the war, so in a sense, women were drafted too—taking positions that had previously been occupied by men. It's estimated that during the war, six million women worked in factories, three million volunteered with the Red Cross, and over two hundred thousand served in the military in special women's branches (although these branches were restricted from combat zones). When the men came home at the end of the war, so did the women. Many women wanted to keep their jobs and their new-found economic and social independence, but the end of the war meant less demand for materials, and the jobs that remained were given to the returning men. Nearly all women were laid off and sent home, the Cult of Domesticity defining women's lives and roles once again.[8]

It wasn't until the 1970s that women truly entered the workforce en masse. But their opportunities were still limited to "pink collar" roles—jobs that were thought to be a good fit for women's temperaments and abilities (fragile and limited).[9] And it was assumed that as soon as a woman got married, she'd quit her job and take her place running a home and raising children.

Gradually, over the last several decades, more career paths have opened up to women. Even in fields that are still often associated with men, such as engineering and computer programming, women are starting to make inroads (although women still earn 17 percent less than men do for the exact same job—and the pay gap is even larger for women of color).[10]

So, why the history lesson? What does this have to do with us today? Everything. It has everything to do with us today.

We're Pushed and Pulled by Historical Precedent

When we make important decisions about our lives, we're often deeply influenced by our historical and societal context, but it can be hard to identify all the ways that context affects us. It's like walking in the ocean—you can't see the undertow, but you can feel that it's there, pushing you this way, pulling you that way, threatening to knock you over or wash you out to sea. Similarly, when we try to make decisions about our career, marriage, and kids, we're making those decisions with hundreds of years of precedent pulling at our ankles.

The idea that an ideal woman should demonstrate piety, purity, submission, and domesticity may sound archaic to some, but for others, that may be the definition of success they've spent their lives pursuing. This isn't ancient history; it still impacts the attitudes and behaviors of women (and toward women) today—myself included.

So many of us feel intense pressure to find our person and get married. Now, of course, some of that pressure comes from our own desires for romance and connection and someone to share our lives with. These are beautiful desires that are baked into many of our hearts. But also, some of the pressure comes from the fact that for centuries, marriage was the only option for women. A woman would live with her father until she found a husband (or a husband was found for her), and then she would move into her husband's house. Marriage was how a woman stayed safe in the world, how she was provided for and taken care of, how she found a home.

When my husband and I first started talking about having kids, the first thing I said was that I loved my career and did not want to be a stay-at-home mom. I had a specific picture of what life as a stay-at-home mom would be like (largely influenced by the Cult of Domesticity, little did I know), and I knew I didn't want that. I could not picture a life where I was supposed to wear an apron and have dinner on the table by six o'clock, bake home-made cookies for every school function, be the perfect hostess, and keep the perfect home. I also did not want to wake up one day as the default primary parent. I wanted to share the role—and I still do! Yet, even after years of conversations about prioritizing both of our careers and raising our kids together, and now years of actually doing it, whenever something goes wrong, whenever our childcare plan gets even the tiniest bit shaky, I immediately find myself offering to quit my job and stay home with our kids. It's not what I want, but it's what women have done for centuries, it's what many of our moms did, and it's what many of my friends are doing—whether or not that's what they want either. I don't want to give up my career, even temporarily. I don't want to be a stay-at-home mom—and that's never been the best financial option for our family—yet it's a role I find myself instinctively volunteering for, as if an unseen tide is pulling me in that direction whether I want it to or not.

Things Are Changing

For much of history, success for a woman has been defined as being a wife, a mom, and a homemaker. And for many women, this expectation still stands today. In many circles, these ideals aren't just general guidelines or preferences—they're moral and spiritual dogma.

While these expectations fit some women like their favorite gardening gloves, they fit other women like shapewear that's a size too small—you can squeeze into them for a while, but three bites into dinner and you're seriously considering ditching them in the ladies' room trash can (not that any of us have ever done such a thing).

For generations, these expectations have squashed the life out of many women. They've forced them to be someone they're not, to take on roles they don't want to take, and to live lives that don't fit.

In a lot of circles, these expectations for women have changed, but that hasn't necessarily made life easier. In an attempt to spring women from the kitchen, from their homes, and from the roles and responsibilities of motherhood, in some parts of society the pendulum has swung all the way to the other side. Women are told that marriage is old-fashioned, and if they want to be a stay-at-home mom, there's something wrong with them for not "wanting more for themselves."

This leaves a different group of women feeling locked out of their lives. They want to be married, they want to have children, and they genuinely don't want to work outside the home. But now they feel like they have to. Once again, women are being pushed into lives that don't fit who they are or what they want.

Other women (like me!) find themselves in the middle. They grew up hearing they could be anything they wanted, and now they're paralyzed by the feeling that if they *can* do anything, they *should* do everything. They want to wear a lot of different hats, and they feel the freedom to do that, but the expectations that come along with all those hats can start to feel heavy. They're trying to do everything all at the same time (that's called "balance," right?) and they're exhausted.

If you're feeling this right now, you're sitting on the tip of the iceberg here, sister. But the good news is that you're not alone.

Things have changed and they're continuing to. More and more, women are fighting for seats at the table and making the important decisions for their own lives. We have options available to us that our foremothers could not have even begun to imagine. But because we're some of the first women with such a wide range of options to choose from, it can sometimes feel like we're building the plane as we're flying it.

CHAPTER FOUR

BUILDING THE PLANE

The number of potential roles available to women in society has increased tremendously over the last fifty years. But over the last twenty years—even the last ten years—the increase has been tectonic. We have more freedom and more options today than women in any other generation. The world is our oyster in a way it hasn't been for many women before us.

Today, marriage is simply an option for women, instead of the only option. While life as a single woman is far from easy, it's possible now in a way it wasn't in the past. Today, women have almost equal access to loans and credit cards, as well as the ability to inherit, own property, and work in almost any field. It's also safer and more socially acceptable than it ever has been for a woman to travel or live alone.[1]

The FDA also approved the birth control pill in 1960, giving women a whole new level of say in whether they wanted to have kids, and when.[2] And there are more options today than ever before for women who want to have babies of their own—with or without a partner.

Speaking of partners, people are getting married later than ever (the average age of first-time marriage for women was twenty-two in 1980, twenty-five in 2000, and twenty-eight in 2023).[3] The process of finding a potential spouse has changed dramatically too. Instead of being limited to people in our immediate circle, we have seemingly endless prospects quite literally at our fingertips.

Women have more options once they're married too. Between 1970 and 2010, the percentage of married women in the labor market rose from 40 percent to 61 percent.[4] In my grandparents' and even my parents' generations, it was common for women to work while they were single and quit their jobs after their wedding, but that's no longer the case. Women are able to pursue both marriage and a career. They don't have to choose between one and the other.[5]

Also, within partnerships, it's becoming more culturally normative for men to take on some of their household's domestic load, which has the potential to create margin for their partners (although statistically, women still carry most of the domestic load, even if they're the primary breadwinner). So while we're not there yet (and it's still incredibly difficult), we have made major strides in women's ability to create a life they love—whether that includes marriage, kids, a career, or all three.

The internet has also added a whole new layer of options. The rise of the internet sparked a new type of industrial revolution, creating types of jobs that were previously unimaginable. It's easier today to start a business than it's ever been before. Not only that, but the Covid-19 pandemic normalized remote work. You no longer have to live in a particular city (or even country) to work there. The new wave of remote positions and hybrid schedules have offered women even more opportunity to customize their lives.

Having all these new freedoms and opportunities is a wonderful thing—and our foremothers fought hard to provide them for us. But the onslaught of options can lead many of us to choice paralysis. Choice paralysis is the idea that the more options we have, the harder it is to make a decision, and the more unsatisfied we'll be with the decision we do eventually make.[6] Having more options doesn't always make life easier. That's something our generation is finding out the hard way.

We're working on a puzzle nobody has put together before, so we don't have many mentors ahead of us who can show us how it's done. The decisions we're making are different from the ones our moms were faced with, so we can't necessarily follow in their footsteps.

First-Generation Working Women

We've been talking about women throughout history—what their lives looked like and what was expected of them. Now let's zoom in a little bit—not looking at history as a whole but instead focusing on your family history. What has life looked like for the women in your family—your mom, and her mom, and her mom? What did they do? What was expected of them? What decisions did they make? What decisions couldn't they make?

Many of us observed the decisions our moms made as we grew up and assumed that's just how things are done. We internalized the timeline of her life and assumed ours would look the same. If your parents got married at twenty-seven, you grew up thinking that's when people get married. If your mom was a stay-at-home mom, wife, and hostess extraordinaire, you imagined you would be too. You'd have four kids, a husband, a house, and an elaborate Thanksgiving tablescape—just like your mom.

(There are also many women who have made it their mission to be nothing like their moms—but even then, our moms are usually the template we're pushing against.)

Having examples to follow and learn from is a gift.

Unfortunately, we often don't see a wide variety of examples of what a beautiful, well-lived life can look like. We don't get to observe an array of lives that are as beautifully diverse as the women who chose them. As a result, we can feel tremendous stress when we get older and realize that our lives can't, won't, or even shouldn't follow the path our mothers' lives did.

Instead of being married with a baby on the way at twenty-seven, maybe you find yourself profoundly single, without even a hint of a relationship in sight. Your life clearly doesn't fit within the template of your mom's life—and without her example to follow, you feel more lost and behind than ever.

Maybe your mom was married with three kids by the time she was your age—a fact that truly boggles your mind. Maybe your mom loved being a stay-at-home mom, but you love your work, and you want to pursue a career outside the home. Maybe you're not sure if you even want to be a mom at all.

Or maybe as you've talked with your mom about how her life unfolded, you've realized that she didn't choose her life as much as it was chosen for her. She had fewer options than you do, and if she'd had more options, she might have chosen differently.

All of this leaves you feeling like you've fallen off the end of the map drawn out by your family history. And because we're charting new territory, sometimes it feels like nobody gets it—like the people who tell millennials that they can't buy a house because they've bought too much avocado toast. You want to grab them by the shoulders and shake them and say, "You don't get it. Things are different now!" And you're right. They don't get it.

They don't get it because we are playing with a whole new set of circumstances and options that have not been available to generations before us. Women in previous generations (even our moms!) were putting together puzzles with fewer pieces and less variation among the overall designs, compared with the puzzles we're putting together today. There were a few specific paths these women's lives could follow, and if they did want to deviate from what was expected, they had to work hard to find those opportunities.

The decisions you watched your mom make, the decisions your grandmother made, those decisions impact how "normal" it feels for you to make one choice or another—that history matters. Just like a first-generation college student, or a person who's part of the first generation of their family to live in a particular country, if you're the first in your family to do something, you have to make things up as you go along. You don't have the benefit of being able to follow in someone else's footsteps.

I'm a third-generation woman in the workforce. My mom is a psychologist, and her mom was a child development researcher. Because of their examples, I felt well equipped to enter the workforce. I actually felt more equipped for a career outside the home than I did for a career inside it. That was fine until my kids were born and I sheepishly admitted to my husband, ten days into their lives, that I still didn't know how to change a diaper. (In my defense, I'd been a little busy healing from a C-section and learning to breastfeed. But trust me, I've had so much practice since then, I could put a diaper on anything.)

But even though I wasn't the first woman in my family to enter the workforce, like many women today I still feel like I've been building the plane as I'm flying it. My mom worked, but her circumstances, options, influences, and pressures were different from mine, so she and other women from her generation don't always know how to weigh in on the problems and decisions I face.

We Don't Have Examples, but We Have Peers—Oh, Do We Have Peers

Comparison (and the insecurity it drags along with it) might be the toughest part of our Everything Era. We're trying so hard, putting ourselves out there, desperately hoping we're not going to fail. It would be easier if we could look at the women to our right and left and see that we're on track and normal—or at least that everyone else feels as lost as we do. We may not be in the same place our sisters or our moms were when they were our age, but certainly we're all in it together when it comes to our peers. Right? Wrong.

The thing is, you've walked in lockstep with your friends for most of your life—you started kindergarten, learned to read in elementary school, wrestled with algebra in middle school, and eventually decided where you'd go to college. And sure, some of your circumstances and experiences may have differed, but in many ways, you hit the same milestones around the same time, and there was safety in that.

But somewhere around twenty-five, things change. Women's lives can look a zillion different ways, especially by our late twenties and thirties—and they do.

It's totally normal for a woman in her thirties to have a high-powered, high-paying career that she loves. It's also totally normal for a woman to be in school in her thirties, or starting a brand-new career. It's totally normal for a thirty-year-old woman to be making a cozy, happy home with her husband and kids. It's also completely normal for her to be renting an apartment with friends, or living with her parents to both help them out and save money. It's totally normal for a woman in her thirties to be changing her youngest kid's last diaper—she's done with the baby phase forever. It's also totally normal for a woman in her thirties to think she might want to have kids someday but have no clue when or what that might look like for her.

This is a particularly lonely season of life for this exact reason. You're navigating something wild and foreign, and instead of having a slew of sisters around you saying, "You too? Ugh, this is hard!" you're trying to talk to your best friend about your dating life while she's trying to get her newborn baby to eat. You feel bad talking to her about what you're going through, and you also feel like she cannot possibly understand. And she feels the same way. It's a lonely feeling.

For the first time in our lives, there is no one "normal." And this is unsettling. We're peeking to our right and left, trying to figure out if we're on the right track, and the answer always feels like "no."

For all these reasons, comparison is one of the hardest challenges our generation faces—and social media has not made it any easier.

When you're on social media feeling extra tender about a specific area of life, it often feels like all you can see are the people who are "ahead" of you. When you're single, everyone seems to be posting engagement photos. When you're trying to get pregnant, it feels like baby announcements are everywhere. When you're feeling lost or stuck in your career, it seems like everywhere you turn, someone is getting a great opportunity or a promotion.

Social media didn't become part of our everyday lives until the early 2000s. Before then, our comparisons were reserved for the people we saw on a regular basis, like the Joneses next door. Did Susan get a new car? I think she did! I heard Bob got a promotion and they're going to take an extra vacation this year. Lucky ducks!

But now, the Joneses are literally everybody. Social media gives us a window into billions of people's lives—a constant slideshow of other people's peak life experiences, perfectly photographed, ruthlessly curated, and expertly edited. And you don't have to hide in a bush to peer into these people's windows either. You can see their highlight reels right from your bed, or while you're in the bathroom or standing in line for your coffee. With each flick of your finger, a new stream of photos makes it painfully clear that these people are where you want to be, and you, well . . . aren't.

This Is Exhausting, but Here's the Good News

This is exhausting. The decisions we face during these years are important and complicated and hard to make. We're trying to figure out so many pieces of our lives all at the same time. And as we do this—as we figure out where we're going to live, and how we're going to pay for it, and if we want to quit our jobs, and what we could possibly do instead, and as we're going on a bunch of second dates that never end up turning into relationships, and as we're trying to figure out if we want to be a mom and if we even *can* be a mom, or if we want to have another kid and if we can afford to . . . we need people on our team.

What we don't need is people watching from the sidelines critiquing our methods or telling us that we need to hurry up. (Looking at you, Aunt Sharons of the world!) We need people in our corner, cheering us on and chanting our name. We need people to remind us that we're smart and strong and that we can do this. And we also need some help along the way as we try to figure out where we're going in life and start taking the steps to get there. That's where we're headed next.

Here's the good news: We grow up thinking that life is a puzzle, with a right and a wrong way to put the pieces together. But the truth is, our adult lives aren't puzzles to complete. They're collages to create.

Your life is like a big blank canvas, and how you fill it is up to you. This can be overwhelming, certainly, but it's also beautiful. Imagine thousands of colorful pictures at your fingertips, each representing pieces of the life that can be yours. You can choose the pictures that inspire you the most, that fit with your dreams, your goals, and your personality; you can ditch the rest. It's up to you how they fit together, how much space you make for each one, which pictures get to take up permanent residence in your life, and which ones get to stay for a season.

And here's the best news: Once you realize there's no right answer and therefore no wrong answer, making decisions about your life can be an incredibly beautiful, fun, and exciting process, as you create a masterpiece and a life that's all your own.

CHAPTER FIVE

YOU GET TO DECIDE

One of the biggest decisions I've ever made was "Am I going to marry this guy?"

"This guy"—also known as Carl Wilson, my husband of almost a decade—and I had started dating not long before I asked myself that question, but it only took a few weeks for both of us to realize we'd found something special.

Carl had also backpacked around the world for a year after college and had moved to north Georgia to work in the marketing department of the nonprofit that put the trip together. A few weeks after I came back from my own trip run by this nonprofit, I did the exact same thing—moved to north Georgia to work in the marketing department.

On a chilly October evening just a few weeks after I started my new job, Carl and I went on our first date. We started talking about marriage just six weeks later.

Carl was the funniest, smartest, most wonderful human I had ever met (still is!). We'd both done a significant amount of personal growth before meeting each other, we'd both dated a lot, and we got to spend a ton of time together right away—fast-tracking a connection that could have taken months if we were long-distance or had different schedules.

Not only did I want to marry Carl, I wanted to get married in general. I'd always wanted to get married. Marriage was never a "maybe" for me, it was a "Definitely. Yes, please. ASAP!" kind of thing. It took a lot of work and intentionality to keep myself from wasting my single life because I was so focused on marriage. But when I realized the marriage thing was actually happening, like right now, I got scared.

One day I was innocently filing away wedding ideas for a relationship I didn't have, and the next I was deciding whether to spend the rest of my life with the person I was currently dating—and finding that the decision was much easier in theory. *I know he's amazing, but is he "the one"?*

It was like in drivers ed where you watch a few videos, do a simulation, and drive around some cones in your high school parking lot, and then, before you know it, you're in a real-life car merging onto the highway. You're like, "Wait a minute, what are we doing? I'm not licensed for this!" The fact that your instructor thinks you're ready doesn't give you any more confidence; it just makes you question their competence.

Half of me was head over heels in love. I was floating giddily around town like the main character at the end of a romantic comedy. But the other half of me was freaking out, fumbling for the exit. My fear grew and grew until I was in an all-out panic. I wasn't just nervous. I didn't just have cold feet. I was petrified that I was going to marry the wrong person and screw up my life.

I'd made big decisions before this moment—abandoning my newly minted journalism degree in favor of an unpaid job in college ministry, backpacking the world for a year doing humanitarian work (which is how I started the blog that ended up starting my career), moving from my home in Colorado to north Georgia (where I didn't know a soul) to work for that humanitarian organization (which is how I first met Carl).

But deciding who to spend the rest of my life with—it

was the most high-stakes decision I'd ever made. Honestly, it probably still is.

When I was trying to figure out if Carl was "the one," everyone around me had thoughts. Tons of couples in our circle of friends were getting engaged around that time, and we fielded questions almost every day about when Carl was going to pop the question. Not only were we dating, getting to know each other, and talking about our future, but we were doing it in front of an audience.

And the audience had thoughts.

My best friend thought we were rushing things and encouraged us to give ourselves some time. (Wise advice. We did exactly that.) My parents asked thoughtful questions about how we were going to support ourselves (fair), but didn't take a hard stance. In my extended family, it was normal to date and live with someone for years before ever talking about marriage, so we were *way* early for their timeline. My boss made sure to tell me his thoughts. (Thanks for that!) He didn't think Carl was a good fit for me. (He was wrong.) Random married couples, upon hearing that we were dating and talking about marriage, would warn us seriously, "Marriage is hard." (I was never sure what to do with that input.) As the cherry on top of this sundae of expert opinions, I found a blog from a couple who had gotten married just a few months after meeting each other. We became friends, so I asked for their advice. They said, "We say, the earlier the better!" They ended up getting divorced just a few years later.

One day during this season, I was sitting with a friend, running through my pros and cons list for the thousandth time. I was trying to figure out if Carl was the one. Every important factor I could think of was ping-ponging through my mind— everything I knew about myself, everything I knew about Carl and our relationship, and all the advice I'd been given along the way. I was panicking—I felt like I was making the most permanent decision of my life so far, one that truly had the power to make or break my life, and I had no idea how to move forward.

I was about to dive into yet another round of "what ifs" when she stopped me. She put her hands on my shoulders, looked me straight in the eyes, and practically shook me as she said, *"Stephanie, you get to decide."*

Those words changed my life.

That day, I learned that a beautiful life isn't one-size-fits-all. This is *my* life, and it can (and should!) look the way *I* want it to look.

The same is true for you.

You get to ask and answer questions like, "What do I really want? What will bring me joy? What do I want my life to feel like on the inside—not just look like on the outside? What kind of future do I want to build, and who do I want to build it with?"

This is true with who you marry, what career path you pursue, if and when you decide to have children, how you choose to create a home . . . *you get to decide.*

No path is perfect. Every option has some good and some hard aspects, and it's up to you what specific combination of good and hard you're willing to live with.

The same was true of the question before me: Did I want to spend my life with the wonderful, imperfect person that is Carl Wilson? If there was no exact right answer, no perfect answer, if I got to decide, then I decided *yes.* And it was truly the best decision I've ever made.

But the power of my friend's words stretched way beyond the decision of whether or not I wanted to marry Carl. Those words changed everything for me. They've become my mantra, the words I've whispered to myself at every turning point ever since. Carl and I say these words to each other all the time, and they help us approach our life—the big decisions and the little ones too—with a combination of creativity and authority that I've discovered leads to a truly authentic life. That day, with four simple words, my dear friend changed my life. Those words gave me a sense of permission that unlocked everything.

Friend, these words are true for you too. When it comes to the important decisions you're facing today, or the big decisions you'll be making next month or next year, you get to decide. You don't have to forfeit things that are good and true about you in an attempt to squeeze yourself into a life you don't actually want to live. Your life should be a beautiful reflection of the woman who chose it. This is your life. You get to decide.

Wait, Is This Really Up to Me?

Screech, halt, wait a minute, stop the music. "What do you *mean* I have authority over my life? What do you *mean* this is *my call*?"

The idea that we have authority over our own lives might feel far-fetched, or even blasphemous to some of us. So, let's pause here and talk about it.

Most of us have spent years, maybe even our whole lives, under other people's authority or trying to please people other than ourselves—parents, teachers, pastors, mentors, or bosses. Perhaps you've felt like you had to follow someone else's lead for most of your life. Maybe you've felt tied to the way things have always been done in your family, town, or church. The rules might be explicit, or they might be unspoken but no less understood. No one is forcing you to do anything, but you get the feeling that if you want to stay at the table, stay connected, and stay included, you need to do things the way they've always been done.

Or maybe you have a parent, sibling, or mentor who loves you and wants the best for you, but who has specific ideas about what that should look like. And maybe you've always felt like you have to get their permission, or at the very least, their blessing, before you make a decision.

Maybe there's someone in your life whose approval you've been working to earn for as long as you can remember. You walk on eggshells around them and consider their opinion constantly—diligently striving to meet their expectations at every turn. You consistently come up short, but that doesn't keep you from trying. You can't imagine a world where their voice isn't your compass.

But here's a hard truth. Just because people have strong opinions about the right way to live a life doesn't mean they're right. It doesn't mean their way is the only way, and it doesn't mean it's the only way (or the right way) for you.

There's no one right way to build a life. A beautiful life isn't one-size-fits-all. It can't possibly be. Everyone is different. We all have different brains, personalities, abilities, desires, values, and circumstances. What works for your sister may not work for you. What works for you may not work for me. We're all holding different sets of cards. You're playing Spades, I'm playing Phase 10—we're two different people playing two different games, and winning will look different for each of us.

Yes, certain life choices may be more popular and more socially acceptable in your circle than others—but what's popular and socially acceptable changes based on where you are and who you're with.

There might be a right way and a wrong way to do life

according to your family, church community, or town—but if you were born into a different family, or went to a different church (sometimes even just down the street), or lived in a different town, the rules and expectations could be completely different.

The ideal woman my friends and I were all trying to be as sorority girls and college students in Boulder, Colorado, was completely different from the perfect new mom in Nashville, Tennessee (the one I currently try not to compare myself to!).

The year I backpacked around the world, I went to twelve different countries, from eastern Europe to eastern Africa to southeast Asia. Each country had its own language, culture, and cuisine, and definitely its own code of conduct—particularly for women. But they were different everywhere I went.

Here's my point: The rules about what it looks like to be a good woman and live a good life can feel binding. They can feel absolute and unbreakable. But if they can change so drastically based on your season of life, your age, or even your zip code, are they truly as absolute and universal as they feel?

Are they rules or trends? Are they doctrines or preferences? Are they a mandate or an option?

I think they're an option. I believe that if we let ever-changing standards of what other people say it means to be an ideal woman dictate how we feel about ourselves, how we spend our time, and what uncomfortable box we shove ourselves into— we're going to waste our lives.

So instead of trying to figure out who the world wants us to be and how we can squeeze, shove, and contort ourselves into that exact mold, let's figure out who *we* are, what makes us *us*, and then be the people we are with our whole heart.

Instead of building a life that some people will think is amazing and other people will think falls hopelessly short, let's spend our time building a life we actually want to live. A life we feel at home in.

I'm not saying that you should indiscriminately throw out the rule book, your family, your friends, or any advice they might have for you along the way. No way. Life is too hard and too important to do alone. I could not be more strongly in favor of having a team of advisors to walk with you through life.

But we're not talking about advice. We're talking about authority.

Do We *Really* Have Authority?

It's scary to be responsible for our lives. We're not sure if we're strong enough, tough enough, or smart enough to wield that kind of authority. Maybe we're ready to pay for our own car insurance, but we don't know if we're ready to sit in the driver's seat for our major life decisions (and there's *no way* we're going off-roading). And that's one reason we sometimes hand our authority over to others or delay taking it in the first place.

Another reason we might shrink away from making certain life decisions is fear of what we may lose if we do—the respect of our parents, a certain role in our friend group, a position in our community. If we're eliminating options out of fear of what others will think, we've ultimately decided we're not in authority over our lives. They are.

I understand this struggle. I'm the queen of the peacemakers, the people pleasers, the appeasers—and that's putting it lightly. But after years in therapy learning about boundaries and how to practice them, here's what I know:

You *do* have authority over your life. What you decide to do and how you decide to do it, those are both within your realm of control. You can give that control over to someone else, but make no mistake, you're giving it away. Except for in extreme situations (usually involving abuse of some kind), another person cannot take your authority from you.

So, what you decide to do, that part is up to you. What happens next isn't.

If someone decides to distance themselves from you, or exclude you, or even punish you in some way because you've made a certain decision, that is up to them. That's the decision they're making, and there may not be a whole lot you can do about it.

But you didn't cause their reaction by making your decision—they chose it.

They could have chosen to respect your authority over your own life, to trust your insight and your boundaries, to support you in doing what you believe is good and right and best for you—even if they disagree with or don't understand some of your choices. That's what we hope the people closest to us do. That's what they do if they're healthy individuals who love us and who are for us. That's what people do if they're truly on our side.

We want our friends, communities, teams, and families to value our voices, care about our needs, and support our dreams. Having opinions—having hopes and dreams and desires and goals for our lives—is not a problem, it's a good thing. If the thing our inner circle values most about us is our silence and our obedience—*that's* a problem.

But maybe it's not another person's authority you've been trying to quietly tuck yourself under. Maybe it's a higher authority. A much, much higher authority.

Does God Have a Plan for My Life?

If you've spent much of your life in church, this part's for you. In faith communities, we spend a lot of time talking about what God wants us to do. It makes sense for people of faith to seek out supernatural wisdom—we're asking big questions about our lives, and we want to get it right. We don't want to step outside God's will for our lives. Being outside God's will sounds like driving a car without insurance: it might be fine, but it could also be a total disaster, and there's no way we're about to roll the dice.

We don't want our risk of failure, rejection, or a broken heart to be any greater than it has to be, and we feel like if we can just figure out what God's saying and follow his instructions perfectly, we'll come out of this okay. He'll take care of us, right?

Yes. He will. I believe he will—but here's where things get tricky.

God taking care of us doesn't mean he's going to wrap us in bubble wrap. God loves you and is with you—and you can still get your heart broken. Both can be true. One peek at the Bible is enough to show you that following God doesn't mean you'll live a life without pain.

In fact, Jesus promised Christians the exact opposite. A life of faith isn't easy, it isn't cushy, and whoever said that we should only make decisions we have peace about needs to either clarify what peace is supposed to feel like or else take another look at the decisions people had to make in Scripture. Our scriptural forebears may have felt supernatural peace at times, but it was certainly often mixed in with discomfort and total terror. (Cut to Jesus sweating blood in the garden before he was crucified.)

But here's the truth we can rest on: God might not put us in a padded bubble, but he will be with us when we get hurt. And that's way better, right? If we lived in a bubble, we'd miss out on the best parts of life—and the best parts hurt sometimes, don't they? (Pursuing our dreams, falling in love, having a baby—those things all *definitely* go in that category). There's no life without death, no love without loss, no hope without disappointment, no success without failure. If you want to experience one, you have to risk the other.

So, back to figuring out what God wants us to do.

If you're anything like me, when you're really stuck trying to figure out an aspect of your future, you pray about it. You gather up all the details of your situation and ceremoniously dump them in a pile in front of God: "Here's what's happening . . . what should I do?" Then, you wait—eagerly looking up to the heavens (or at your bedroom ceiling) hoping for a direct answer or a pain-free three-step plan to be revealed. But it rarely works that way. So when that doesn't work, you'll go to church or to a pastor or spiritual mentor and see if they know what God wants you to do. But that gets tricky too. Because while the advice you get from them might be good and God-inspired, it's going to have some of their perspective mixed in as well.

Whenever a pastor preaches a sermon or even meets you for coffee, they're taking God's Word and helping you understand what it means and how to apply it. That's super helpful. The reality, though, is that while the pastor is teaching from the Bible, their teaching will also be shaped by their own perspective, knowledge, and personal experiences. So when you look back over the notes you diligently took during the sermon or jotted down on a napkin at the coffee shop, you might have some truth and wisdom from God there, but you'll also likely have some thoughts and opinions from your pastor mixed in alongside. That's not a bad thing, you just need to remember that and act accordingly.

Your college pastor may have taught specific principles about singleness and dating and marriage. These principles may have worked well for him and for many other people in your community. But just because he had great ideas doesn't mean he's the one and only authority on relationships, or the source of indisputable truth about what God wants you to do in any relationship situation you may face. Yet that's what it sometimes feels like, doesn't it? Opinions we've heard and respected for years can be hard to shake.

There are some decisions I've made in my life—as well as some decisions I didn't make but felt guilty for not making— because of advice I was given by a pastor or spiritual mentor. In these situations, I sometimes felt like I was either following or disobeying God himself. But that's not what was happening. The truth is, I was either taking or rejecting the advice of another human—a smart, well-meaning person who was doing their best to represent God. But that's different from hearing from God himself.

So, knowing how easy it is for human voices to get mixed up with God's, in many seasons of life I've looked to the Bible directly to tell me what to do. I've scoured Scripture, looking for a specific answer to whatever problem I was facing—but I could never seem to find it. I either had to find two dots that I could creatively connect and make up an answer of my own, or I walked away frustrated. Occasionally I would even treat my Bible like a Magic 8 Ball. I'd ask a question, close my eyes, flip to a random page and poke my finger down. Whatever verse my finger landed on, that was my answer. That last technique was particularly unhelpful. Surprising, right?

The Bible is a sacred expression of God—full of wisdom and guidance for those who seek it. It's an epic story of a God who loves his people and who is on a mission to bring them close to him. It's not a Magic 8 Ball. And we get tripped up when we treat it that way.

We run into trouble whenever we start looking for God's specific instruction on something the Bible doesn't actually give specific instructions about. We're studying an ancient text, trying to figure out if we should or shouldn't go on another date with this guy, and the Bible just doesn't seem to be answering the question.

It's not that God doesn't ever have specific answers for us. There are some things God is crystal clear about. But that doesn't often include where he wants us to go to college, how many dates we should go on, which job he wants us to take between two equally good options, or which house he wants us to buy when we're looking at several options with similar size, location, and price point.

I'm just not sure that he cares.

Don't get me wrong, I think he cares about a lot of things. And he cares about us. But I just don't know that God's will for our lives is as specific or easy to fall out of as we imagine—not even with our biggest life decisions.

I think God looks at two houses, two jobs, two cities, two different potential spouses even, and says, "Yep, I can totally work with that. I am in both places. Neither is outside of my love, my provision, or my will. What do you want to do?"

Now, if you're anything like me, you don't love this idea. It sounds easier and safer to have God slam every door shut except for the one that's going to lead to joy and comfort from now until forever. But I just don't think God works that way. Part of the process of creating a life you love is embracing the authority you've been trying to give to God—but which God actually intended to give to you.

So then how do we move forward?

Sometimes, even after looking for answers, we still come out unsure. Some people will speak with certainty—saying they see definitive direction in Paul's letters for which internet-based start-up you should work for. You can follow their convictions if you want to, but I'd rather see you follow yours. After a lot of trial and error, I've made it a personal policy that I'm not going to sign myself up for a life I don't want to live just because someone told me that's what God says I'm supposed to do.

Nowadays, I talk to God myself, and I encourage you to do the same. Get to know him. Spend time with him, talk to him, learn about his heart and his character. Ask him what you should do, and know that often the answer is, "It's up to you, kiddo. But know that I'll be right there with you either way."

There's a Frederick Buechner quote I just love:

> The place God calls you to is the place where your deep gladness and the world's deep hunger meet.[1]

Deep gladness is not selfish, inconsequential, or unrelated to God's plans for our lives—rather, it's an indicator. It's a clue to the type of life and decisions we're specifically designed for. It may seem too good to be true, but God's glory and our joy often intersect. So when you're facing a decision, examine what it is that you want to do, what lights you up, what makes you feel excited, which option—imperfect as it might be—you want to live with.

And then make the best decision you can, knowing that even if you screw it up God's still going to love you. My conviction is that there's very little (if anything) you can do to screw up your life beyond his ability to repair or redeem.

What Happens If We Don't Embrace Our Authority?

It's important to embrace your authority because you are, without a doubt, the most influential person in your life. You are in charge. The calls are yours to make.

Not only do you have authority over your life, but if you want to create a life you love, you're going to have to start making some decisions—and making them now. If you don't intentionally figure out what's important to you and make choices accordingly, life and time and other people will choose for you. Maybe you'll still end up somewhere you want to be. But approaching life this way is like throwing a dart with your eyes closed. If you hit the bull's-eye, it's because you were uncommonly lucky. It's much more likely that you'll end up with regrets.

If you don't make decisions now, you might find yourself stuck in indecision for so long that you never build a life at all. The inertia that comes with not knowing what you want may cause you to miss your chance to build it. And while life sometimes offers us extra time and second chances, some opportunities may only be available to you in this season. If you don't take them now, you might not ever get to.

There are other areas of life that work like an investment account or a fine wine—they grow, mature, and get better with time. You can wait and get started on these things further down the road if you want to, but there's a lot to be gained if you start early.

The biggest risk of all is that you might end up living a life you never actually wanted. You might find yourself shuffled along through the years, guided by what other people say you should do without ever stopping to take inventory of where you want to go and what you need to do to get there. You might successfully build a life that looks nothing like you and doesn't feel anything like you hoped it would. You might end up living out someone else's dream instead of your own.

Here's the truth: Very few people accidentally stumble into a life they love. If you want to build a life you love, you need to do it on purpose. You need to figure out where you want to go and start taking steps in that direction, but where you go and how you go about getting there is up to you. There's a lot of room for creativity.

Have you ever heard of the Camino de Santiago? It's an ancient pilgrimage through France and Spain. It dates back to the ninth century, and people have been making the arduous journey ever since. It ends in a beautiful Spanish city called Santiago de Compostela, where, allegedly, the remains of St. James are buried in the town cathedral.

People do the Camino for all kinds of reasons: they need space to think, a fresh start, a challenge, to get away. But most of them are hoping for a deeper connection with themselves, God, or both.

There are more than 450 rest stops, or *albergues*, on the Camino. Albergues are homes or hostels just for pilgrims, offering them food, a shower, and a place to sleep. The albergues are often hosted by families who have been doing this work for generations.

The thing that's so fascinating about the Camino is that it's not just one specific path. For ancient pilgrims, the journey to the cathedral began on their doorstep. There wasn't one designated starting point or route, and there still isn't. The only requirement to receive your "Compostela" (your certificate of completion) is to document your last one hundred kilometers.

Camino means "the road" or "the way" in Spanish—and yet it's not one road, and there's not one way.

This is true about building a beautiful life as well. There's not one right way to do it. There's not one right path. You don't have to stop and take a rest whenever anyone else does along the way. Your experience will be different from those of the other pilgrims, but it should be—because you are different, your circumstances are different, and what you need out of your experience is different too.

Many different roads can lead to a beautiful life—you just have to decide which one is right for you.

And that's exactly what we're about to do.

CHAPTER SIX

AUTHORITY AND CREATIVITY

There's no exact recipe for building a life you love, but if there was, it would certainly call for generous amounts of both authority and creativity.

Authority says, there are all kinds of decisions I could make about my future, and I get to choose the right one for myself. It's about valuing authenticity above people-pleasing. Sometimes you may find yourself in lockstep with the way things have always been done in your family or community, and other times you may end up living in a way that seems foreign or even countercultural to the people around you. Authority means being okay with that—trusting your voice and your insight above the opinions of casual onlookers who aren't the ones who will be living with the consequences of your choices, anyway.

Authority means taking your rightful place as the leading lady of your life and taking responsibility for the decisions that are yours to make. It means making all the individual choices that will make up your life—a life you actually want to live in.

That's the goal here. You're not making perfect decisions, you're making decisions you can live with—decisions you *want* to live with. And only you have the authority to do that.

Creativity, on the other hand, means believing that there are all kinds of ways to put a life together. Creativity knows that a beautiful life isn't one-size-fits-all, and it commits to both seeking out and trying different ways of doing things until you find something that works—not just for other people but for you. Creativity means being willing to step outside the box—or, even better, to take the box and turn it into something else entirely, just like we did as kids. Sometimes creativity leads us far away from convention, and sometimes it just puts a little twist on it.

Our lives aren't puzzles. The goal isn't a series of "right" answers, those satisfying clicks when two pieces fit together exactly the way they're supposed to. Most of the time, there *is* no "supposed to." Instead, we get to cut and paste and glue and rearrange and thoughtfully assemble the pieces of our lives just the way we want them.

This process is empowering and fun—but it can also be a bit overwhelming and intangible. So here's a practical example.

Creating a Home You Love

The most expensive decision many of us will ever make is the decision to purchase a home. It's a huge financial commitment. If you buy a home, it will likely be the most expensive line item in your budget for the next thirty years, and it will impact how you spend your time as well. When you buy a home, you're committing many (many, many, many!) hours to its care and upkeep. Your choice of home can also have a significant impact on your quality of life. In buying a home, you're selecting the conveniences you want to have every day—and also the frustrations you're willing to live with.

But beyond the logistics, your home sets the stage for the life you're going to live inside it—in fact, it *is* the stage. Your home will be the backdrop for the best moments of your life, the hardest moments of your life, and all the little moments in between, and therefore it should fit your real needs and priorities, not just the current trendy list of must-haves.

For example, Carl and I have always loved the idea of a long, beautiful dining table—so we've had one for years. It's perfect for elaborate dinner parties, and when we first got married, I was convinced we'd be the elaborate dinner party kind of people. It turns out, we're not, especially not in this season of life. When we have people over, we're much more the crowd around the island people—curl up on the couch people—hang out in the kitchen and sit on the barstools people.

Also, I'm way more of an apps and drinks and dessert person than I am a four-course meal person—especially if I'm cooking it (which I almost never do).

So for years, our large dining table has sat in our dining room, mostly unused (though often holding mail or packages waiting to be returned)—a reminder of a life we aren't actually living and don't even want to live right now. It's become a relic, recalling dreams and priorities from a different season of our lives.

Then last year, we received a small bouncy house in the mail. We didn't order it, it wasn't a gift, it truly was sent to us by mistake. And that made it hard to return. Finally, the customer service rep we were talking to suggested we donate it or just throw it away.

We definitely weren't going to throw it away, and before we donated it, we might as well try it out, right?

The first time we used it, it was a super hot day here in Tennessee—far too hot to go outside. We needed a way to keep our kids occupied, and we needed something fast.

In a flash of creativity and authority, I had an idea.

We pushed our big table to the side of our dining room and used the newly open space to blow up the small bouncy house.

Why not turn our dining room into a playroom? Why not have a bouncy house inside? Instead of having our dining room sit vacant waiting for a dinner party, why not use it for something else in the meantime? It didn't have to be permanent. Or, it could be! Why not?

My girls *loved* it, and so did I. It was such an empowering moment for me—I got to see how our house could—and should—be a reflection of our family: who we were, what we wanted, and what we needed in that season of life. And all that can change. It should change.

I broke "the rules" by putting the bouncy house in our dining room, and I was surprised at how good it felt. When we create a beautiful home according to someone else's standards and opinions, we end up caring for, paying for, and maintaining a home that is right for somebody else but not necessarily right for us. And that zaps us of the time, energy, and freedom to create something that would have worked better for us.

A home is an enormous expense and a huge commitment. The more home (and stuff) we have, the more time we spend taking care of it. Unfortunately, many of us end up spending our time and money in ways we didn't consciously consent to—that we didn't actively choose. Before we know it, we're spending most of our time and money maintaining things that aren't actually life-giving for us. It's draining.

The point is, you get to choose. You get to create a home that works for *you*. Your dream home is *your* dream home. Your home is the setting for your life, your family, your work, your rest, your dreaming, your community, and so much more. Your home is where you spend your life—so you should like it.

There are no rules for creating a home. If plants are what makes you feel the most inspired, the most alive, the most connected to your best self, then you can live in a greenhouse. You can have as many plants as you can make work in your home.

Or you can thrift everything in your house. You can furnish your home with repurposed materials. You can go on a hunt for household items made in the 1950s, if that's an era that inspires you. You can live super minimally in a small space and spend most of your life out in the world. Or you can buy a bigger house and spend most of your time inside.

It's up to you. It's up to me. And the more I take hold of my authority, the more I open up my options wide and think about them with creativity, the more fun life starts to be, and the more authentically I live it.

Our homes are a practical, tangible example. But this creative, personalized way of living is possible in every corner of your life. Your career, for example: you can work from eight to five every day in the same office for the entirety of your career, or you can have three part-time jobs that allow you to do different types of work in different locations each day.

One job doesn't "count" any more or less than another. As long as you have the means to house, feed, and clothe yourself and anyone else you're responsible for, it counts. If it's working for you, it works.

And yes, some people might award you extra points for having a career that's traditional or impressive by their standards—but what are those points worth? What can those points buy you? Certainly not rent or a vacation or day-to-day satisfaction or enjoyment of your work.

Those extra points might pay off at your high school reunion or at a dinner with your extended family, but they don't count for much more than that. So why would you spend your entire life trying to earn them?

This principle applies to your relationships too. Friendships, partnerships, marriage—they're not one-size-fits-all. Each relationship is unique, because both people in any relationship have their own unique needs, lives, preferences, and circumstances. You can build your relationships around the unique factors each person brings to the table.

My husband, Carl, and I teach an online course for engaged couples and newlyweds, and "Are we doing this right?" is one of the most common questions we're asked. ("Are we having enough sex or having sex the right way? Is this the way you're supposed to share a closet? Can we do our own thing a few nights a week or should we be spending every evening together? Do we need to go to bed at the same time?") Our answer is always the same: "What do *you* want? What do *you* need? What works for *you*?" The answers to those questions are going to be different for everybody.

When Carl and I got married, the first bit of advice I remember receiving was, "Make sure you go to bed at the same time every night. That's the key to a happy marriage." We tried for a while. We really did. But he's a night owl and I need as much sleep as I can possibly get, so in trying to force ourselves into the same schedule, we were both miserable. It wasn't until we remembered that *we* get to decide, that we did just that—we put together a schedule and a rhythm that works for us as individuals and for us as a couple. (Usually, this means that I head to bed at nine while Carl stays up until midnight or later, and our best quality time happens in the evenings. I get plenty of sleep, he gets good introvert time—it works great for both of us!)

You get to do this too. Just because your mom was in charge of one household chore and your dad was in charge of another doesn't mean you have to wedge yourselves into those roles and responsibilities in your marriage. Just because your friends handle things a certain way in their marriage doesn't mean you have to do the same.

This principle holds true in all our relationships. Some friendships work best with constant communication, while others thrive on a once-a-year meet up. And what works best often changes as we grow. The rhythm we had with our roommates in college isn't likely to work the same ten years later.

Some people call their mom every day, others see her for Sunday dinner every week, and others see her a few weekends every year with plenty of texts and calls in between.

In your relationships, you and the other person involved are the decision-makers and the most important judges. You get to try something new and then ask yourselves, "Does this work for us? Is this good for our relationship?" And your answer matters. Other people's opinions, at the end of the day, really don't. And your answers may change depending on your season. Something that worked for you in one season of life may need to shift as you enter another.

Creating a life you love is a process of thoughtfully reimagining your life and doing so as often as you need to or want to. It can involve absorbing wisdom and asking for advice, absolutely, but it's important to filter that advice through the lens of what you need today and where you want to go tomorrow.

So, how do we actually *do* that? That's where we're headed next.

PART TWO

BUT HOW

DO I DO IT?

CHAPTER SEVEN

GET FREE

The four little words "You get to decide" set me free, and I hope they do for you too. But they might also immediately raise the question, "Okay, but how?"

Imagine that you're sitting at a crossroads. You know you need to move forward, but you're not sure which road to take. Maybe you're trying to figure out if you want to stay at your current company or try something new, or if you're ready to start trying to get pregnant, or if it's time to move to a new city.

Hearing that you have the authority to make the decision is exciting and empowering—for like, two seconds. Then it's overwhelming, because if you're responsible for the decision, you're also responsible for the outcome. It would almost feel easier not to have a say. If you don't try, you can't fail. If you don't put yourself out there, you can't be rejected. If you don't make a decision, you can't make the wrong one. And if you base your decision on what someone else told you to do, you can always blame them if it goes wrong.

Having authority is also overwhelming because it seems like the second you are told that you get to do what you want, you realize, "Oh my gosh, I don't know what I want." You've been so caught up in everyone else's expectations, you've never figured out your own.

Ever since I heard the words "You get to decide," I've been trying to figure out how. *How* do I decide? How do I make these life-altering decisions? How do I create a life that looks and feels like me, a life I'm excited about and proud of, a life I truly love?

Through a lot of research, a lot of trial and error, and a lot of practice, I've figured out a process that has helped me make the biggest and best decisions of my life.

You can use this three-part process whether you're looking at your life overall, a specific area of your life, or one specific decision.

Here are the three parts we'll unpack together:

Get Free
Get Inspired
Get Moving

Let's Get Started

When we come to a fork in the road in our lives, we never show up empty-handed. We show up carrying societal expectations, expectations based on what our family has always told us we're supposed to do, expectations we formed because of what we saw our friends doing, or even expectations we internalized because of a passing comment someone made one time that somehow just stuck. Even if we don't ask for anyone else's input, we still have it. We somehow know on a deep, cellular level what different people think we should do.

Do I Want to Be a Mom?

Six months after our wedding, Carl and I took a trip to the Dominican Republic with his family.

I stretched out on a beach chair as I looked out at the ocean.

I could see Carl and his brother in the water a few yards out, throwing a football back and forth.

I was reaching for my book—slightly soggy from damp hands and sunscreen—when a family walked by in front of our chairs. A dad chased after a giggling toddler, and a mom shielded her new baby from the sun as she adjusted the baby carrier she had strapped to her chest.

The kids were adorable, and my sister-in-law saw them too. She leaned over from the chair beside me and gave me a poke. "Steph, when are you and Carl going to give me a niece or nephew?" she said with a wink.

She was teasing, being sweet. She was expressing nothing more than her excitement for our future and her joy at being part of it. For a moment, I caught her excitement. I felt warm and happy at the thought of being able to give our families a baby to love.

But as quickly as it had arrived, the excitement faded.

Because on the heels of it came a new realization:

I have arrived at the point in life when people expect me to have kids. This is the age. This is the stage of life. And not only are people expecting it, but biologically, if we want to have kids at some point, we probably need to do it soon.

Maybe it sounds silly, but this was a brand-new thought for me.

I'd always assumed I'd have kids someday, but I didn't think "someday" would arrive so soon.

Before that day, I wasn't thinking about kids. I was thinking about my new husband and our new marriage and our new apartment and getting settled in our new city. I was thinking about work and what I wanted to do with my life and trying to take steps in that direction.

There was so much to figure out already. And that day, a whole new set of questions dropped into my lap.

Did I want to be a mom? Now that the possibility was close by instead of far off in the future, I honestly wasn't sure. What did it mean to be a mom? What would my life as a mom look like? Was that the kind of life I wanted to live? What would being a mom do to our marriage, my career, my body, my ability to pursue the other dreams and goals I had for my life?

Was I ready to be a parent? And what does *ready* look like anyway? Was I qualified to create and raise another human? I sincerely doubted it. And with the world feeling so messy and divided and scary, the thought of bringing a little human into the chaos felt, I don't know . . . a bit irresponsible?

I had a thousand questions and no clue how to find the answers. This was such a huge decision—how did anyone make it?

The question of kids loomed over me for the rest of our vacation. Each night I would wake up with a start at four in the morning, consumed by anxiety, feeling like I had to make a decision right this second, and having no idea how to do that.

And unfortunately, that anxiety tucked itself into my carry-on and came home with Carl and me from the Dominican Republic, taking up residence as our new (and very annoying) roommate.

I wrestled with this question for years—actual years. *Do I want to have kids? Do I want to be a mom? And if so, when?*

I didn't necessarily feel like I had to have kids, and I also didn't feel like I had to have them early. My mom, busy getting her doctorate in psychology, had me at thirty-four and my sister at thirty-seven. My parents always told us how valuable they'd found it to have some years to just be married before we came along.

Nobody in my life was telling me I *had* to have kids, but still, I felt like someone somewhere had said we were supposed to have kids—and for some reason I felt like I had to comply. Even harder for me to overcome was the idea that if we were going to have kids, it was supposed to look a certain way. (And I did not like the picture in my head one bit.)

Despite the fact that my own mom hadn't done this, I assumed that I would have to become a stay-at-home mom if we had kids—that no matter what we talked about, or what I actually wanted, I would become the default parent, a hundred percent in charge of my kids, leaving zero percent left over for anything else I might want to do with my life.

I was also told, expressly and repeatedly, that Carl and I should travel now, because once we had kids we wouldn't be able to. I began to resent my nonexistent children before I was even sure I was going to try to have them.

I wasn't ready to say no, to write off the idea of ever becoming a mom. But I was *not* ready to say yes. I felt like I had to live my whole life before my kids came along, because as soon as they did, it would be over.

But then one day, Carl repeated the words that have changed my life over and over again: "Steph, we get to decide." He was right. I began to unpack some of the messages I'd been believing about parenthood, unwinding some of the "supposed-tos" that had me twisted up inside.

Unexamined expectations are kind of like a giant tangle of yarn—a confusing mess, with lots of different colors and textures knotted together. The only way to sort through them is to put the big knot out on the table in front of us and pull at the threads until we figure out where each of them is coming from. Looking at a certain thread, you might say, "Wait—I've been living as though this has to be true, but where did this come from?" Until we untangle the expectations and decide how we want to respond to them, we live under their pressure and power. Once we isolate and examine each expectation, we can decide whether we trust the source—and if we want it to be a guiding force in our lives or if we want to intentionally do something different.

Let's talk about the different types of expectations we should be on the lookout for in our lives—because until we identify them, we can't crawl out from under them. There's something powerful about naming things—wrapping words around what we've felt but never been able to describe. So let's start there. For our purposes, I think there are three main categories of expectations.

EXPLICIT EXPECTATIONS

These are expectations that have been directly given to you, either once or repeatedly as you were growing up:

You will go to college.

Everyone in our family has studied medicine and you will too.

When you take over the family business . . .

I never got to stay at home with my kids,
*   so I want you to be able to.*

With explicit expectations, you understand clearly what's being asked of you, who's doing the asking, and how much is at stake if you fall short or take an alternate route.

74

IMPLICIT EXPECTATIONS

The word "implicit" feels particularly poignant here because it means "implied although not plainly expressed," and it can also mean "without qualification or question; absolute."

Those definitions perfectly capture the slippery nature of the implicit expectations we all face. Nobody has told us that we have to do things this way, but they don't have to. We know what's expected of us—and the expectation is absolute.

For many people, marriage is an implicit expectation. Few of us are explicitly told, "You have to get married, and you have to do it by this age." But when that's what everyone around us seems to have done, it feels like we have to do it too. Finding the right person and getting married becomes not an "if" but a "when," and we spend our childhood and adolescent years talking about, dreaming about, and preparing for this inevitable aspect of our future.

If there's a certain way things have always been done in your town, community, family, or church, that's often an implicit expectation. When you've watched people meeting the unspoken expectation for many years, it's hard to imagine a different way. It's hard to dream of something you've never seen—but we'll talk more about that soon.

I once knew a couple who walked into marriage with opposite sets of implicit expectations about their future family structure. The husband, born and raised on the West Coast, always expected that his wife would have a job outside the home. Where he grew up, it was considered old-fashioned to expect a woman to be a stay-at-home mom. His wife, on the other hand, grew up in a particularly conservative area of the South. Where she grew up, it was expected that a woman would be a stay-at-home mom. And if she *had* to work outside the home, that should be

75

downplayed because it signaled that her husband wasn't able to fully support his family.

This couple was so entrenched in the implicit expectations they'd both grown up with, it took them quite a while to figure out what was right for their family.

You can spot an implicit expectation by the way people talk about those who don't meet it. "She's still single, bless her heart." "She's going to be the oldest mom at preschool at this rate. Oh, I'm just kidding." As if "bless her heart" and "I'm just kidding" do anything to make the words less hurtful.

And implicit expectations aren't even the trickiest kind. That award goes to assumed expectations.

ASSUMED EXPECTATIONS

Assumed expectations are sneakier than the other two categories, but they're no less powerful.

Assumed expectations are expectations that nobody in your life directly puts on you, either explicitly or implicitly, but you carry the weight of them anyway. You assume other people expect these things from you, often because you've internalized the expectations that have been placed on other people. I do this a lot.

I have a friend whose mom put a lot of pressure on her to stay at home with her kids. To her mom, working outside the home equaled being a bad parent. "The best place for your kids to be is with you," her mom said to her, "and you're harming them if you leave them with anyone else." Even though my friend told me about this just one time, that's all it took.

I assumed that expectation—I borrowed it, picked it up, and felt the weight of it. I assumed that it was what the people in my life thought I should do too, even if that wasn't actually the case.

It was this expectation that almost kept me from having kids. I assumed that if I had kids, I would have to spend every moment with them—sacrificing all the other parts of my life that I'd worked so hard to cultivate, the things that make me *me*.

I held on to that expectation, living under the pressure of it for years. Assumed expectations are tricky that way—they're the sneakiest kind, so they're the hardest to escape.

Untangling Our Expectations

Before we can make a decision of our own, we have to figure out what we think we're *supposed* to do, and why. We need to quiet the outside voices, wherever they came from, before we have even a prayer of hearing our own. We must stop and examine the expectations we're living under—pulling at each thread until we find the origin.

After a particularly stressful conversation about the future of our family, Carl said, "Steph, I don't understand. Why do you think your life is over once we have kids? You can still have a life. You're not going to be doing this by yourself."

"Yes, I am!" I shot back. "If I'm going to be a good mom, I'm going to have to be with my kids every hour of every day. No babysitters, no backup, it's just going to be me. When in the world will there be time for anything else?"

His face was incredulous. "Where did you get that idea? Who told you you *had* to be with your kids every second of every day to be a good mom?"

I sat back on the couch, quieted by his question. Truthfully, I wasn't sure. I searched my memory, thought about conversations I'd had with friends who had gone before me, various mentors I'd had over the years, things I'd read, shows I'd watched—I couldn't find anything. I'd asked a few people in my life for input, but none of them had told me anything close to that. In fact, they'd all told me the opposite—that it's good and healthy for kids to spend time with other safe adults, that prioritizing your health and well-being as a mom is essential to raising healthy, happy kids. My own mom worked outside the home and I *loved* our babysitters. They were wonderful and fun, and they were such great mentors for me growing up. Where had I picked up this pressure?

Finally, I remembered the conversation I'd had with my friend. Her mom thought she was a bad mom for going to work and leaving her kids with a babysitter. Her mom would think I was a bad mom for doing the same. Her mom had given her that pressure, and I'd picked it up and carried it too. I'd been carrying it around for years.

But it wasn't until Carl asked that question that I realized whose voice I'd been listening to.

I was ignoring the advice of the most important women in my life, not to mention the books and articles I'd read from childhood development experts and psychologists, all because of something my friend's mom (who I have never met) said one time, not to me, but to *her*.

Friend, we have to figure out who we're listening to, because only then can we examine the source of our expectations and decide if they're actually what *we* want, or if we just *think* we're supposed to want them. Let's start by identifying your outside voices, figuring out what they're saying and who's saying it, and taking a look at what they're telling you to do.

We'll do this with two main questions.

1. What Do You Think You're Supposed to Do?

Before we can decide what we want our lives to look like in a specific area, we need to look at what we think our lives are *supposed to* look like in this area. Admittedly, this can be hard to do. It's hard to see something that's always been there, that's faded into the background and become part of the furniture. So, if you're having trouble seeing what expectations you might be bringing into your decision-making process, think about the decision you're trying to make and run it through a few of the following prompts. You can do this whether you're trying to make a specific choice or whether there's a part of your life you're wanting to reimagine.

My family would be so happy if I _____

_____.

When my mom was my age, she _____

_____.

I'm supposed to want _____

_____.

I feel like my only option is to _____

_____.

When I picture my future, I can only imagine _____

_____.

Everyone else is _____

_____.

I should _____
_____.

I'm supposed to _____
_____.

Good women always _____
_____.

Pay attention to how you're feeling as you respond to these prompts. How's your breathing? What's happening with your shoulders? Are they relaxed or are they way up by your ears? What's happening in your stomach? Is your heart beating fast or slow? Do you feel relaxed and supported and excited about some of the options that come to mind for your life? Or do some of them make you feel anxious, stressed, or even trapped? Pay attention to how each option makes you feel—to what your body has to say about it.

2. Does It Have to Be That Way?

Here's the next question, and it's equally important: Does it have to be that way?

Sometimes I've been living under an expectation for so long, I am honestly not sure. *Do I have to do it this way? I think so . . . right? Don't I?*

To figure out if an expectation is one I need to meet, I find it helpful to tease it out a little bit. A question I often start with is, "*Who* told me it had to be this way?" It's important to cite our sources!

Once you've answered that question, examine the source. Who is this person? Is it someone close to you or someone on the fringe of your circle? Do you trust them? Is it someone who deeply knows you and your circumstances and all the facts, or someone making a casual comment that just happened to hit home?

Or maybe your answer to the original question is broader, something like, "the internet" or "my church" or "my family" or "society and culture." But if you can, try to get a little more specific than that. Are there certain voices on the internet that seem to be driving this message home for you? Did someone at church make a comment that you latched onto and internalized? Maybe it's a social group or a political party or a subset of a political party (or a few extra-loud members) who are vocal about a certain topic—and it's their voices in your head that are setting this expectation.

If the source of your expectation is more of a group like this, see if you can designate a group representative. Whose face do you picture when you think about this group and the expectation you feel like they're setting for you? Let that person be the representative for this particular expectation.

It takes an extra moment or two to take these mental steps, but it will make the next part much clearer.

Now that you're thinking about the person who set this expectation for your life—whether it's someone you know or a representative of a group—think through their qualifications. Is this someone who you've given permission to speak directly into your life? Is this someone you want to take advice from? Do they have all the information? Are they an expert—someone who is specifically equipped to weigh in on a decision like this? What does their track record look like in their own life when it comes to this particular subject? Do you trust this person—are they fully on your team? Are they impartial, or do they have a horse in this race? Did they put a lot of thought into their recommendation, or was this something they just threw out there? More than once, I've taken an offhanded comment someone didn't even remember making and—without even realizing what I was doing—structured my life around it. Here's an embarrassing example:

You know how in some restaurants they have a kind of billboard on the backs of the bathroom doors? They might sell ad space there, or they might post information about their latest happy hour offering or their Easter brunch plans—taking advantage of the attention of their captive audience, of course. Or sometimes they post other random fun stuff there, like a funny poem or a list of fun facts.

It was on the back of a restaurant bathroom door, probably fifteen years ago, that I saw a fun fact that really stuck with me. It said, "Right-handed people live an average of nine years longer than left-handed people."

That was the fact. It was squished between two other random facts, but because this one wasn't so fun (it felt pretty morbid, actually), it stuck with me. I distinctly remember feeling grateful for my right-handedness, and sad for everyone in the world who was left-handed.

I'm sure I thought to myself at the time, "Why is this? What does being right-handed or left-handed have to do with life expectancy?" But instead of looking into it further, I moved on, ordered dinner, and promptly forgot about it.

Only I didn't exactly forget about it. That fact tucked itself away and has lived in the back of my mind ever since. (It's back there with my best friend's landline phone number, my first boyfriend's birthday, and the lyrics to "Party in the USA".)

Fast-forward to a few years ago when my daughters were

born. As they got a little older, we started to notice that they were both favoring their left sides. If they were going to kick a ball, they'd do it with their left foot. When they'd pick up a spoon or a crayon, they'd use their left hand.

The more this pattern emerged, the more upset I got. It wasn't a conscious upset—it was more like a low-level hum of resistance to the idea that they might be left-handed.

Finally, in a conversation about them kicking a ball with their left feet, it all came spilling out. I told Carl that I didn't want our girls to be left-handed, because life expectancy for left-handed people is nine years shorter than it is for right-handed people.

Carl said, "Wait, what? Where did you hear that? There's no way that's true!"

As soon as I heard the words "a bathroom flier" tumble out of my mouth, the realization of how ridiculous this whole thing was hit me like a tidal wave. I didn't even need to look back at Carl's face to know that he was looking at me like, "Are you kidding me?"

Now, of course, I eventually looked it up, and yes, there was an article in a reputable scientific journal in the 1980s that made this claim, but the study was based on a skewed sample and there's no truth to it at all. Thank goodness.

The reason I told you this story is not just so you can laugh at me (although feel free to do so). I told you this story because we do this kind of thing all the time, and it's rarely as benign as my debunked "fact" about left-handedness. We hear an opinion or questionable statement from someone, whether a friend or family member or a stranger on social media, and if we don't recognize it and challenge it, we could potentially carry it around for years, letting it wiggle into our subconscious and change the contours of how we live our lives.

Asking the "who" question is a crucial step. Who told you this was true or that it had to be this way? Is it someone you know and trust? Is it someone who was trying to give you thoughtful, intentional advice? Is it someone who knows what they're talking about?

Unless we pause and ask these questions every so often, we might find ourselves worrying about something we saw on a bathroom flier one time. Or maybe that's just me.

Now, maybe the person who gave you advice was right. Maybe you didn't like what they said or how they said it or the fact that the advice they dispensed was totally unsolicited. But they might have been right. And even though it might take you a minute to get there, eventually you may feel grateful for the dose of reality they dumped over your head—because it would have been worse to miss an opportunity or make a decision you end up regretting because you had your information wrong.

But also, even if they are right, if what they said is true, there's likely still wiggle room. Now you get to ask questions like, "How true *is* this? How heavily should I weigh this new information? If they are right, is their way the only right way to do it? Or is there a work-around?"

Finding a Work-Around

After years of pros and cons and back and forth and asking questions and changing our answers a thousand times, Carl and I decided we did want to be parents.

The way we got there—the way I got there—was partly by examining the expectations I thought were on me as a woman, the implicit and assumed expectations I was carrying around that told me that I had to have kids because it's what women do.

But I gained even more freedom by examining my expectations of what motherhood was going to be like. I had an initial mental picture of how motherhood would be, how it *had* to be, and how I had to be in it. And it turns out, none of those expectations was correct. I thought that once a woman had kids, she automatically had to have a bunch, and she also had to quit her job, drive a minivan, never travel again, lose all her friends, and only ever talk about diaper cream and food allergies—and none of that is true.

We get to do this *our* way. Moms come in all shapes and sizes. And thank goodness for that!

Also, admittedly, I was too hard on minivans. While I don't currently have a minivan, I have no longer ruled it out, because my friends have since educated me as to the error of my ways. If you're carting around a crew of kids, a minivan is definitely the most comfortable and convenient way to do it. My best friend, Kelsey, has a red one she named Stacy—and Stacy usually has nineties rap music bumping from her speakers.

The more I looked around at the actual women in my life and saw how they were parenting in many different ways that were beautiful and specifically suited to them, the more I was able to see that there was room for me to do the same.

A huge shift happened for me when I read a book about a family who took their three children on a yearlong trip around the world. So many people had told me that we couldn't travel once we had kids—as if they make you exchange your passport for your baby's birth certificate on your way out of the hospital. But this book showed me that that's not true. Kids can travel too.

The more I realized that I could approach motherhood and our family's day-to-day life with the same authority and creativity I'd brought to all my other decisions, the more I started to get excited about the prospect. I didn't have to do this someone else's way, I could do it *my* way—and not only would that be okay, but it would be better. My daughters don't need the quintessential supermom, they need *me*. Bringing my whole self into motherhood isn't impossible—it's actually imperative for our success as a family.

But I didn't know that until I saw real examples of women doing motherhood differently. Now that I'd quieted the unhelpful outside voices, I had to incorporate some better ones.

CHAPTER EIGHT

GET INSPIRED

Now that we've liberated ourselves from the cacophony of unhelpful voices in our lives, it's time to incorporate some more helpful ones. Life is too hard and too important to do all by ourselves.

Many of us grow up believing that asking for help is weakness, but I could not disagree more. While it's crucial to evaluate the voices speaking into our lives, we do need people in our corner if we're going to create lives we love. You can't possibly be good at everything or know everything. If you truly want the best possible outcome, you need to assemble the best possible team. You need people you trust on your team and in your corner. You need coaches, a council, a board of directors, advisors. I've always thought about these people in my life as my cabinet.

Your Cabinet

If you're a politics buff (or love *The West Wing* as much as I do), you're familiar with the idea of the president's cabinet. The cabinet is an advisory group made up of the president's closest confidants. According to the White House's website, "The Cabinet's role is to advise the President on any subject he or she may require relating to the duties of each member's respective office."[1]

A small group of your closest confidants who are there to advise you on subjects about which they have particular expertise? Yep, love that.

I love the expectation behind the idea of the cabinet. Nobody's expecting the president to be an expert on everything or to do everything by themselves. That's not the measure of success, because that's not actually possible. How could one person have deep knowledge and wisdom about the wide array of issues that require the president's attention and action every single day? It's just not possible, and because that's the case, success is instead measured by the president's ability to form a team—to bring in the best advisors in all different areas to help them fill this massive role.

We need a team around us too. This *waves wildly to everything* is just too much. The quantity and variety of decisions I'm going to have to make before noon today is just too much. I cannot possibly be an expert on everything, and you can't either. But the good news is, I don't have to be, and neither do you. We get to have help from all kinds of experts around us.

Sometimes we just need a quick question answered. It's a onetime thing, a question the internet and the bazillion smart people it connects us to can answer.

But our cabinets are more personal, more intimate, more consistent and involved. They're the people we trust most, the people who know us best, the people we go to for advice knowing that they're going to guide us in a way that truly makes us better and leads us closer to where we want to go.

One of the most important things we can do in The Everything Era is to gather people around us to help us through it.

How to Create Your Cabinet

I'm talking about cabinets as if they have a set number of people with formal titles and specific jobs, but it doesn't have to be like that. It doesn't have to be formal. You don't have to ask people to join it, and they don't get a badge or a certificate for saying yes. Putting your cabinet together is more of an internal process. It's a chance for you to intentionally decide who you're going to listen to and what you're going to listen to them about—to match your areas of need with the people you have in your life to help.

Years ago I sat on my therapist's couch, anxious about the prospect of motherhood and how it would impact my career. I went on and on about the different possible outcomes of the Choose Your Own Adventure book I was imagining in my head: if I choose to do this, that limits my options to these, and what if I don't like either of those? I talked for several minutes before my very wise, very kind therapist leaned forward and said, "Can you think of anyone in your life who is doing it the way you'd like to do it? Is there anyone navigating that season well who you could look to for some additional wisdom?"

It was a game-changing conversation. A name popped into my head immediately, and, while it didn't magically take away my need to make some decisions and moves, it calmed my inner panic to know that, yes, in fact, I did have people to look to and turn to.

Take a moment to consider this in your own life. What are your current challenges, and can you think of any potential sources of wisdom in your circles, whether it's someone in your closest circle of friends and family or, more often, someone from your wider circle of acquaintances and friends-of-friends? Who has a solid track record in their own life? Who is working through their own seasons with the kind of authenticity and intentionality you want to emulate?

If you know you're struggling at work, but you don't have any friends or mentors who are ahead of you in your career field, you need to find someone who is. You have a hole to fill in your cabinet. Or if you're looking to grow and heal mentally and emotionally, it's important to have someone who can walk you through that process. (Ideally, this should be someone who really knows what they're doing. And remember, even if you're a therapist, therapists still need therapists!) If you're stepping into a new season of life, whether marriage or motherhood or another new role, having women in your corner who have been there and made it through will make your journey a thousand times easier.

Thinking through who *is* in your cabinet will also help you discover who isn't. Once you know that, it makes unsolicited advice from the Aunt Sharons of the world much easier to take with a grain of salt and then politely discard.

And again, you don't need to formally ask someone to be in your cabinet. If you have access to the person and are able to ask them personal questions every so often, that counts. Some members of my cabinet—usually my best friends—I talk to almost every day. Other members of my cabinet, my therapist for example, I currently talk to less frequently, perhaps once a month. They're all important, they're all wildly helpful, but they help me with different areas of my life in different seasons of my life and so I need them at different intervals.

Let's talk about numbers: how many people should be in your cabinet? Well, the president's cabinet has fifteen people. I have about fifteen in mine too, but I'm a person who really likes input. (Sometimes to my detriment. I can easily end up with too many cooks in the kitchen.) In your cabinet, you can have as many people as you want, as many as are helpful to you. But two good guidelines are to make sure you have enough—enough support to help you through the decisions you're navigating right now—and make sure you have enough variety. Nobody is good at everything, so while your best friend is amazing, she may not be the person you want advising you on your dating life, and your job search, and your finances—particularly if she's not great with those things. You want to ensure you have the support and counsel you need in a variety of different areas of your life. Far more than a number, that's really the thing you're looking for.

You might be wondering what makes a person a good fit for your cabinet. What qualities should you be looking for?

Our cabinets should be made of people who are close to us, people we trust, people who care about us enough to learn and remember the details of our lives. They have specific experience and expertise that have given them deep wisdom in the areas where we need help. They have great track records in these particular areas of their own life. They're also impartial. They're not trying to convince us to do one thing or another. And they put a lot of thought and effort into the recommendations they give us.

I'm big on citing sources, so I also want to know that the people I'm listening to are listening to other voices I trust. Here's an example:

A dear friend of mine, Emily, is brilliant and wise and I have her weigh in on all kinds of things. One of her favorite topics, and therefore one of my favorite things to ask her about, is current events. Emily has a way of gathering information about what's going on in the world and distilling the complexities into a text message that helps me quickly get up to speed and also truly grasp what's happening. I love this about her. I trust Emily, and when she tells me something, I believe her. Part of the reason I trust her is that I also know and trust her sources. Emily's not getting her information through rumors on the social media grapevine. Her headlines aren't coming from the tabloids at the checkout counter. And she's not easily persuaded by misinformation. She's a critical thinker who asks good questions and seeks reputable sources, and because of that, she's become a trusted and reputable source for me.

Another thing I look for in a person before I ask for or take their advice is whether their values are similar to mine— whether they're walking in the direction I want to go. I've been a business owner for the last twelve years, and I love learning from other business owners who are further down the road than me. But before I start taking someone's advice, I always try to assess their values. I'm not interested in following in the footsteps of someone who never sees their family because they're working around the clock. That's just not the type of success I'm looking to emulate. It doesn't mean I won't listen to anything they have to say—I'll just run their advice through an extra filter, knowing I might have to tweak their suggestions to better fit the things that are important to me.

Life is too hard and too important to try to do it alone, so make sure you have people in your corner to help you along the way. But also, make sure they're the right people. Before you decide to follow someone, make sure they're headed where you want to go.

Get Inspired

In the last chapter you had a chance to examine what you feel like you're *supposed* to want (and shake off some of that pressure!). Now that we've talked about which voices you're going to listen to—and which you're not—it's time to figure out what you *actually* want.

This can be hard. Have you ever had someone ask you what you want for your birthday and your mind instantly goes blank?

You knew the answer right before they asked the question, but now that you're on the spot, you're frozen.

Knowing what you want in life can be this way too.

It's great to be reminded (or have the first-time realization) that you don't have to want something you always thought you had to want. But that just tells you what your destination *isn't*. It doesn't tell you anything about what it is.

So how do you figure out what you want in life? Yowza. You're going to need a minute. You might also need some inspiration. Just as we talked about with implicit expectations, many of us have seen one main life trajectory lived out over and over by the people around us for all of our lives. Or maybe we've seen a small array of options, but they were all within the same color palette—"You have to paint your bedroom pink, but you can choose from these four shades of pink!"

As we discussed in an earlier chapter, women entered the workforce in droves in the 1970s, but for a long time, their career choices were limited. What if a woman didn't want to be a nurse or a teacher or a secretary? What if she wanted to be an astronaut or an entrepreneur or an acupuncturist or an artist? It's hard to paint with colors you don't know exist, so if the people around you all seem to be following the same few paths, it's going to take a massive amount of creativity to both imagine and engineer a future you have no context for.

This is one of the (many!) reasons why representation is important. It's hard to be what you've never seen. So, let's find some inspiration.

We're going to do this in two ways. First, we're going to look outside—we're going to seek out a wide variety of examples of what life can look like. There's no pressure. We're not making any decisions just yet; we're simply browsing. The more options we see available, the more creative we can be when making decisions for ourselves.

Then we're going to look inside. Many of us don't know what we want because we've never truly asked ourselves. And maybe when we have thought about it, we've felt conflicted. "Well, part of me wants this, but part of me wants this other thing."

We're going to talk through all of that.

But first, let's look outside.

LOOK OUTSIDE: WHAT'S AVAILABLE?

Before you figure out what you want to do, let's take some time to look at ideas for what you *could* do. Go wide with this. Seek out as many ways of doing life as possible. All the options certainly aren't going to fit you, but broadening your horizons proves to you that there's not one right way. It also helps you get more creative by giving you new pieces to play with.

You can do this by watching other women make decisions about their lives—watching their process, their choices, the outcomes. Seek out as many different examples as you can find.

Seeing women living differently is important because again, it's hard to be what we've never seen. Our imaginations are wild and beautiful and incredibly powerful, but if we've never seen anyone do something, it's hard to know that option exists. If you've always painted with shades of black and white, and everyone you know has always painted with shades of black and white, that's all you know. You can't imagine painting with a pop of cerulean blue, because you've never seen cerulean blue.

Examples of different ways of living open our eyes to new possibilities, broadening our horizons of what could be. We can pick and choose pieces from other women's lives: "Yes! I want some of that too, and a dash of that, and a pinch of that!" And even if we don't see ideas we'd like to borrow for our own lives, seeing women live differently proves to us that there's not one right way to live a life. It gives us permission to dream bigger, to dream differently. And that makes all the difference.

My friend Mariko has been a huge inspiration to me for years. As a parent, she marches to the beat of her own drum, following her own inner compass about what's right for her and her kids and what just isn't that important. For a rule follower like me, this approach feels revolutionary, and while I wanted to adopt it immediately, it's taken some time to get the hang of it. "Wait a minute, I don't have to do what everyone else is doing? I can look at what's most important to me and what my kids need and make decisions accordingly?" (I'm telling you, I'm writing the book on this topic, but it's because I've had to learn this lesson over, and over, and over, and over again.)

"Yep," says Mariko, and she does exactly that. Her family's culture, their home, and the decisions they've made over the years are so beautifully *them*. I'm constantly inspired by their example.

Several years ago, Mariko and I were at dinner and she was telling me about a new idea she and her husband were starting to dream about. "It's funny," I remember her saying. "Whenever we have a new dream or a new idea, we always start by joking about it. We say, oh, hey, wouldn't it be funny if we moved to Nashville, or tried to have another kid, or if I went back to work, or if we built a tiny house in our backyard." She described how the other person would always respond, "Yeah, that'd be funny," and then she and her husband would joke about it for a while as they both processed the idea—trying it on for size.

Watching her trace their wild ideas and wonderful plans back to that starting point made me wonder where big ideas start for me, and where they start for me and Carl together. I realized that the seed usually comes from a friend. We'll see someone else living a certain way, pursuing something, or even just thinking about pursuing something, and that plants the idea in our lives too. It's as if we don't realize that thing is an option until someone else shows us that it is, and then we can evaluate it for ourselves, try it on and see if it fits.

Sometimes our friends don't even end up doing the thing they told us about. It wasn't a good fit for them. That's what happened with the trip I took around the world. My friend Jacy mentioned it to me, but she didn't end up going. It wasn't the right next step for her; it wasn't a good fit for her. But it *was* a good fit for me.

A few years ago, our friends Kelsey and Tyler were talking about selling their house. They hadn't outgrown their current house yet, but they thought they might soon, so they'd started to look—not really, not officially, but they were keeping their eyes open.

Later that night, I told Carl what Kelsey and Tyler were talking about, and before I knew it, we were looking too. Kelsey and Tyler didn't end up moving for another year or so, but we moved just a few months later. Their idea sparked something in us, and while it wasn't the right time for them, it was for us, so we took the leap.

As I've watched this pattern happen in my life over and over again, I've become more intentional about watching the way other people live, the decisions other people make. The more variety I see, the more creative I become when making my own decisions. Someone else's idea can spark something new in me, and regardless of what they end up doing with that idea, the seed has been planted in fresh soil in my own heart and life. Suddenly, I don't have to paint with just pink, I have the whole rainbow to choose from—and my palette is expanding all the time.

Where I Look for Inspiration

One of my favorite ways to get inspired is to observe how differently people use their homes. Admittedly, I watch more than my fair share of home design shows, but I just love them. I especially love the shows about people living in crazy, wild, out-of-the-box homes—like a retrofitted firehouse, or a tree house, or a super-narrow home on a tiny plot of land in the middle of a big city. I'm endlessly inspired by these people's creativity. Not only do they give me ideas I never would have thought of on my own for how to structure and design my physical space, but they give me ideas for other areas of my life too. When I see someone take something and transform it into something else, it helps me see that as an option for any obstacle or decision I'm facing.

Whether I'm on the internet, watching TV, out in the world, or talking to a friend, I'm constantly on the lookout for ways women are making life work for themselves. The more ideas and variety I see, the more creative I'm able to get in my own life and the more personalized I'm able to make my decisions.

One area where I'm always looking for inspiration is childcare. It's a huge pain point for many families, so I'm always wondering how people make it work. Some of my friends have their kids in daycare, some have a nanny, and some do a little of both. I have friends who do a nanny-share (where families team up and hire someone together—so the nanny gets the stability of a full-time job, but the families don't have to pay for more time than they need). I have friends who do a childcare swap ("You take all the kids on Tuesdays; I'll take them all on Thursdays"), and friends who stagger their work schedule with their partner's so someone's always there to be with the kids. These families handle their childcare needs in so many different ways, and not only does watching them give me ideas ("Oh, I never considered a childcare swap!"), but it reminds me that there's not one right way to do this. It gives me permission to make the decisions that are right for us.

Food is another area where we can be creative. We all have to eat, but there are a thousand different ways to do it. Some people do meal kits, others do CSAs (a subscription box of food but from a local farmer), and others do a meal swap with another family ("I'll make a double portion and bring you food tonight, you make a double portion and bring us food on Thursday!"). For some people, their kitchen is where they feel most creative and alive—making delicious meals for the people they love. For others, their kitchen is simply a drop zone for takeout containers. Some make dinner for their kids and then eat dinner themselves after the kids go to bed, some prepare elaborate family dinners, and some find themselves eating dinner in the car as they pursue other things that are really important to them. Everyone's getting fed. These are all great options!

We can also get creative when it comes to our cost of living. Housing is a big expense for most of us, but in some cites and economic climates it can feel positively crushing. Many people have found ways to offset some of their living costs, whether by renting out a spare bedroom, building an apartment over their garage (or a tiny house, like Mariko did!), hosting exchange students, taking a job someplace like a university that has on-campus housing included, or even multigenerational living.

These are all beautiful options. If we can think of it, we can do it. But thinking outside the box is hard—that's why we need examples to help.

What about different ideas when it comes to marriage? Carl and I had been dating for a little less than two years before our wedding day. A few weeks ago, I stood up with one of my best friends as she married a wonderful man she's been with for twelve years. You can get married in a courthouse, elope on an island, have a small backyard wedding with close family and friends, or plan a huge blowout wedding with five hundred guests. Every one of those options will get you married, and every one of those options can be beautiful! You get to decide what you want and what you need.

Or how about work? You can work in an office, you can work from home, or you can even do some of both. Or you can work anywhere in the world where you can find good Wi-Fi. You can work full-time or part-time or just a few hours a week. You can work during the day, you can work during the night, or you can work a job that lines up with your kids' school schedule so you can be home every day before they are.

The world can sometimes feel black-and-white, but when I keep my eyes open for all the different ways there are to live, I find that life isn't just shades of gray, it's shades of every color—like standing in front of the wall of paint swatches at the hardware store.

All the options we've described have pros and cons, positives and negatives—and what's a pro for you, may be a con for me, and vice versa. The point is, you get to decide!

It might feel overwhelming to see so many options. We'll talk about narrowing them down in a minute. But before you can make a choice, it's important to see that you really do have a variety of choices you can make.

What to Do with What You Find

As I've gathered inspiration throughout the years, I realized I needed somewhere to put it all. I considered a notebook, a pinboard, and sticky notes, but finally, I decided to create notes on my phone. I like this option because my phone is always with me, which means I'm always ready when inspiration strikes. These notes are a judgment-free zone. No idea is a bad one, and nobody else is ever going to see them anyway. They're just for me.

One of the notes in my phone is called "This is what I want to be about." This note is where I store little clues I find about who I want to be, what I want to be doing, and why. I take notes when something brings me joy—or when something really doesn't. I note what I'm doing when I feel most alive. (Let's do more of that!) And I note the things I'm doing when I feel the most drained. (Less of that, please!)

When I see someone living in a way that's inspiring to me, I write it down. It may be something I've never considered or something I don't think I'd ever do, but something about it appeals to me, even if just a little bit, so I write it down like a clue.

I add to my notes most often at night when I'm trying to fall asleep (that and the shower tend to be the times when ideas come to me the easiest). My practice of writing them down has been a way of pulling the ideas out of my brain, saying to myself, "Yep, I hear you! Great thinking! I promise, I won't forget this! And now, it's time to go to bed—but I'll save this for you for tomorrow." (That's how I talk to my toddlers too. It works well for both of us.)

Then, when I do have time and need some ideas, I can pull out my notes and go through them to find ideas and inspiration at a time when I can actually do something with them!

I might not be able to come up with the answers to my big life questions all at once and on command, but I can gain insight little by little, in the shower, during a conversation with a friend, or while watching something on TV.

And those little moments of revelation really add up.

Over the years, I've spent more and more time looking for women who are breaking the mold—creating lives that look like them and feel like them and work for them. And the more I see, the more I notice, the more empowered I feel to create my own life in a way that's a little different, a little outside the lines, but that looks like me, feels like me, and works for me and my family.

LOOK INSIDE: WHAT DO *YOU* NEED?

So, you've looked at a broad spectrum of possibilities, you've noticed the wide variety of choices others are making, and you feel like you have a good sense for what else could be out there—you've looked outside. Now let's look inside.

Maybe you know exactly what you want—you just need time and space and a reminder that there's no one right way to build a life. You need everyone else to be quiet for half a second so you can hear yourself think, hear your heart speak. And once you have that time and space and distance from all the things you feel like you're supposed to want, your own wants and needs become clear. You just needed someone to put the authority back in your hands: "Hey, don't forget, you get to decide. You can create a life you love."

On the other hand, maybe you have no idea what you want because you shut down your own needs and wants so long ago you've lost touch with yourself. You truly have no clue. Or maybe you've never known what you want and you've never known how to figure it out.

Maybe you're feeling conflicted. Sometimes the loudest competing voices are right in our own minds. Part of us wants one thing, and part of us wants the complete opposite. Who do we listen to in that scenario? We've talked about silencing outside voices so you can finally hear your own—but what happens when your inner voice is arguing with itself? That's the place I usually get stuck. Part of me wants to do this, part of me thinks I should do that, another part of me wants neither, and I have no clue who to listen to. I want to pause here and say that this inner conflict is totally normal. If you're feeling this, you're not crazy or silly or doing this wrong.

Now, I wish there was a simple formula to follow—*Answer these three questions and you'll know what you want to do with your life*. Unfortunately, it's not that simple. Each of us is facing different decisions and different sets of circumstances, and we're arriving at our decision points carrying our own unique collection of desires, past experiences, and hopes for the future.

So instead of a formula, imagine a toolbox. I'm going to share with you a few tools that have helped me make some of the best and most important decisions of my life. One of the tools might speak to you more than the others do today, and that might change tomorrow. Feel free to take what you need and leave the rest for later.

But first, a disclaimer: Some of these exercises might feel a bit woo-woo, but go with me here. Even if you don't have any clear revelations, you're showing yourself a deep kindness by taking time to consider your own goals, wants, and dreams. It's a beautiful and radical act of self-love and self-care.

Aim for Excited and Proud

In the beginning of this book, we talked about creating a life you're excited about and proud of. I chose those two words intentionally because to me, that's what it means to create a life I love.

Creating a life we love isn't about choosing the path of least resistance. We're not trying to skate through life with as much sugary-sweet, surface-level happiness as possible. That's not what we're looking for.

We're looking for deep meaning and connection. We want to

make a difference in the world, to leave things better than we found them. We're ready to do the hard work required to achieve and enjoy the things we've always wanted—even if it takes some blood, sweat, and tears along the way. (On most days, that is. Some days we may wish it was all a little easier.)

But we're not *just* looking to do the hard things. As we talked about earlier, just because something is hard, doesn't mean it's right. Not every difficult journey has a prize at the end of it. Journeys don't have to be grueling to be good.

In seeking to create a life we're proud of, it can be easy to slip into people-pleasing territory. It's easy to conflate what makes *us* proud with what makes *other people* proud. It's easy to glorify the difficult, to assume the hard road is always the best road, but that's not always the case.

That's where the word "excited" comes in. One of the hardest things about being a human is that we have to do it every single day. So, what kind of life could you actually be excited about? What makes you want to get out of bed in the morning? What fills you with purpose and passion? What feels fun? What would transform your days from a "have to" to a "get to"?

Simply building a life we're excited about doesn't quite fit the bill either, though. It doesn't satisfy our deep need for our lives to mean something. You can do a lot of things that are exciting, that sound fun and enjoyable and that you'd look forward to— but if you're not also doing things you're proud of, excitement starts to get hollow after a while.

That's why this section has two different questions for you to consider:

What decision would you be proud of yourself for making?
What decision are you excited about making?

These two questions should ultimately lead you to the same life—they're like a yin and yang, holding each other firmly in balance. Often, building a life you're proud of leads to a life you're excited about, and living a life you're excited about softens and humanizes the drive to make yourself (and other people) proud.

Trying to make decisions I'll be proud of often leads me to longer-term thinking and planning. It reminds me to invest; it reminds me that if I want something to exist in my future, I might need to get started on it today. But trying to make decisions I'm excited about reminds me to live in the present—it keeps me from missing out on my life today because I'm so focused on what I want it to look like tomorrow.

So I invite you to spend some time sitting with those two questions. This may lead you directly to a conclusion. It may make things crystal clear, but it also might not. Either way, it will give you more information about what you want as we move forward. And that's all we need right now.

Dream about Your Life in Five-Year Increments

One of the hardest things about figuring out what we want in life is the reality that life is (hopefully!) long. Filling the next sixty years with dreams and plans feels like packing a giant suitcase without any packing cubes. You're shoving things into nooks and crannies, hoping it all fits, but knowing that you're likely going to have to pull it all out again and organize it. It's overwhelming.

Instead of feeling like you have to plan out your whole life all at once, let's create a set of "packing cubes" for your hopes and dreams. Take some time to journal and dream about future seasons of life in five-year increments. What do you want your life to look and feel like at thirty, thirty-five, forty, forty-five, and beyond?

You don't have to make any decisions as you do this exercise. Your dreams aren't carved in stone. You're dreaming, not making a to-do list. But the process of considering what you want to see in your future can help you set priorities for the years leading up to that.

You can always check in later and change what you came up with, and you can do this as often as you'd like. But the process of thoughtfully looking forward is a beautiful one, and it can have the power to quietly and subtly orient you toward exactly what you're looking for.

Work Backward

The last tool I want to share with you is basically the opposite of the one we just talked about. Instead of starting at the present moment and looking forward at your future, we're going to picture sitting at the end of your life and looking back.

One of the most inspiring women I've ever known was my Gramie. My mom's mom, she was full of life and full of fun, and despite living across the country from us, she felt deeply present in our lives. She was my third parent and my favorite pal. We actually named our daughter Annie after her. Annie is hilarious and already full of creativity and spirit—just like her great-grandmother.

My Gramie passed away a few years ago, right as I was turning thirty, and as I rushed to her bedside during her final days I remember feeling desperate to gather some last words of wisdom. My sister and I asked her, "Gramie, what's important? What do we need to make sure we don't miss?" I knew that at ninety-two, with a full life now almost fully behind her, she had perspective that we couldn't possibly have, and I wanted to hold on to any wisdom she wanted to offer.

She was having a hard time talking by that point, so she kept her words simple. "Talk. Laugh. Take a walk."

I got it. Don't miss the little things. They're what's truly important.

Humans often struggle with the reality of our mortality. It's morbid and terrifying and heartbreaking and mind-bending to imagine that one day you just won't be here anymore.

But if we let it, the fact that we don't live forever can actually be a gift. It reminds us not to miss our lives, not to waste them. It gives us clarity on what's important and what's not.

Now, it's hard to zoom out and see our lives as a whole when we're right smack in the middle of them. It's hard to imagine what we'll want sixty years from now, what will happen between now and then, how the passing years will change us. It feels impossible to predict.

Except . . . is it? When I'm ninety-two and standing toward the end of my life, I can think of some things I will want to have done more of—and some things I'll want to have done less of. I can think of a few things I'll remember vividly and some things I'll want to be able to look back and remember. I may not be able to forecast everything that will happen in my life up to that point, but surely I can know some things that will fall into each of these categories.

So that's the last invitation I have for you as you're looking inward. At the end of your life, what will you be glad you did? What will still be important to you? What will you remember? What do you want to be able to remember? And what simply won't matter?

At the top of my "this won't matter" list is how I look. When I'm ninety-two, I know for a fact that I will wish I'd spent way more time jumping into lakes and oceans and clear, sparkling swimming pools (and swimming in the rain, the way Gramie always taught us to!), and way *less* time worrying about how I look in my bathing suit. It's hard to keep that in mind, but I really, really try.

Define Success for Yourself

Now that you've gathered both inspiration from outside and insight from inside, let's take a few minutes to distill those thoughts down. Don't worry, I'm not about to make you write a vision or mission statement—anyone else dread assignments like that? Just me?

Instead, look at the ideas you gathered from both outside and inside yourself and see if you can identify some themes. What are some of your values, some of the priorities you're pursuing?

Knowing your values and priorities won't necessarily make the choice for you. The logistical questions are still there, and we'll get to those soon.

Here we're talking about how you'll know whether you've succeeded in life. What are you pursuing? How will you know if you get there?

Another reality to consider is that there isn't enough time in the day for you to pursue every possible worthy goal—so it's important to identify your top priorities. Even if you bend over backward trying to do it all, at the end of the day you still end up giving things up—whether it's mental health, sanity, balance in your life, connection with yourself as a human, connection with your spouse, or genuine enjoyment of your kids.

As an example, say one of your priorities is giving your kids a rich childhood, but you've never actually defined what that means to you, so you're scrambling trying to do it all. You're trying to plan fun and interesting craft projects, feed them delicious meals filled with perfectly nutritious foods, and ask them specific questions during dinner to engage their minds and enhance their vocabularies. You're prioritizing good things, but maybe too many good things. You find you're too busy setting up the next craft to sit down and be with them as they work on the first one. You're so busy preparing the perfect meal for them (that they might not eat anyway) and choosing your dinnertime questions that you miss out on their around-the-table banter, the song they just made up, and the look on their face the first time they try a pickle: *Sour? Sweet? I hate it? I love it!*

Now, food and crafts, they might be your thing, and that's great. But my point is, there are a lot of great things you can do with your kids (and with your life!), and there's not going to be time for all of them. We simply cannot be all the things all at the same time. We're going to fall short somehow, so either we choose what we're going to prioritize and what we're going to let go of, or life will choose for us. And since we often fall last on our list of priorities, the thing we let go of is most likely going to be ourselves.

Going back to our example, as a daughter myself, I can say that I'd rather have a mom who's present with me than one who performs for me. I'd rather have a mom who's healthy and happy and loves her life, herself, and being with us, than one who ticks all the supermom boxes.

In my own mothering decisions, I make these types of calculations all the time. Do I care about this? Is this truly important? Or can I let this go?

And here's the important thing: these decisions are going to be different for every mom. The things we value, the things we want to impart to our kids, the ways we want to bring value to their lives, what we keep and what we let go of, it's going to be different for all of us.

Whether our life priority decisions involve motherhood or our careers, marriage or friendships, geographic location or family concerns, passion projects or self-care, we have to define success for ourselves. We have to clearly name what we want to prioritize and what we're willing to give up; otherwise, we're going to kill ourselves trying to do it all or meet someone else's definition of perfection.

You don't need to write a defined list of your priorities right here and now. If you know them, then by all means, write them down and hold on tight. But I'm not asking you to cast a vision for the rest of your life this very moment. Perfectly worded elevator pitch not required!

Figuring out your priorities can be a onetime, sit-down-and-get-it-all-out kind of thing, but it doesn't have to be. Your list can shift and change and be wiggly and imperfect. You can sketch out a detailed vision for your life, or you can carve a few bullet points in stone. Or you can aim for more of a feeling, a guiding sense of how you want your life to be.

I do some of all of the above.

However you decide to come to your answer, the question is this:

What does success look like for you?

Here are some thoughts for you to consider as you answer this for yourself:

I want to make absolutely sure I _____ _____, and in order to make space for that, I'm okay letting go of _____.

Here are a few more questions and prompts to help you unpack your thoughts:

In this area of my life, as I make this specific decision, or in my life in general, what does success look like? How will I know if I've gotten there?

I have limited time on earth, in the world, to spend with my people, to get things done in a day—how do I want to spend my time? What do I want to make sure I achieve, and what things can I let go of?

At the end of my life, I want to look back and know for sure that I did this: _____.

When my partner looks back on the years we've spent together, what I want them to remember is this: _____ _____.

I know that I can't be all things to all people and that because my time and energy are finite, I'm going to have to disappoint someone. The people I want to disappoint as little as possible are _____.

When my kids look back on their childhood, I want them to remember it being _____, and in order to make space for that, I'm okay letting it be

_____.

We've been talking about creating a life you're excited about and proud of. Defining success for myself is how I've been able to do just that. This practice has helped me both find my path and stay on it.

It's helped me be able to say, "Yeah, I may not be doing this your way, but I'm doing it my way and I'm truly proud of the woman I'm becoming."

CHAPTER NINE

GET MOVING

Have you ever cleaned out a messy closet? It's overwhelming, right? There's never a good time to do it. It's always like, sixth on your to-do list—high enough that it puts pressure on you, but low enough that it never actually gets done. You can live with the mess, but it's frustrating and inconvenient. It makes your mornings harder, and every day it whispers to you, "You're falling short, you're a mess, you're not working hard enough, so-and-so's closet doesn't look like this . . ."

If you're anything like me, you might put a date on the calendar: "I'm going to tackle the closet this weekend. It's happening. I'm doing this." But then you arrive at the date and the process of sorting through the mess is so . . . messy! It always seems to get worse before it can ever get better, and you get frustrated and overwhelmed and agitated until finally you say, "Argh, forget it!" and shove everything back into the closet. You'll deal with it another day.

Big life decisions used to feel this way for me. Can you relate? That's why we're going to do this one small step at a time.

But before we do, here's something you should know:

You're not going to screw this up. There's no one perfect answer, so you're not going to miss out on finding it. There's not a right choice, and that means there's not a wrong choice. You just need to take a step forward—and the only way you can screw this up is if you don't. Staying still is the real danger here, the real dream killer.

Staying still means missing out—you miss what could have been, the opportunities you might have gotten, the lessons you would have learned, and the beautiful ways you would have been transformed by choosing something, even if things didn't turn out the way you'd hoped.

The longer you stay still, the harder it is to get moving. The longer you stay still, the more pressure you feel to make your next step perfect. But you don't need to make the exact right next step. You just need to take *a* step.

When you take that step, you open up a new array of possibilities that simply weren't available to you when you were at square one.

And here's the thing: if you don't like where that step takes you, that's okay, you can take a different one. You can change your mind.

It's terrifying to decide something if you think that decision has to be locked in for the rest of your life. But most decisions aren't that way. Most courses of action can be changed—reversed even.

Did you know that only 27 percent of college graduates have a job that is closely related to their major?[1] That means that 73 percent of them study one thing and end up doing something else. Isn't that wild? Now, some people might hear that statistic and think that those college degrees have been rendered useless—that the people who earned them did all that work for nothing, since they didn't end up working in their intended field. But that couldn't be further from the truth.

First of all, whoever thinks we should be bound to the vision for our life that our eighteen-year-old selves picked at college orientation needs to talk to an eighteen-year-old. We had no clue what we were doing. I know I didn't.

We were making the best decision we could with the information we had at the time. And as we got more information, we amended our decisions accordingly. But that doesn't mean the time we spent pursuing our earlier choices was a waste. No matter what you study in college, you're practicing learning new things, you're cultivating discipline, you're learning to work with a variety of people, and you're gaining context about the world—how we got here and where we're going. You're growing up—you're taking your first steps into the adult world, figuring out who you are and who you want to be. All of that is valuable.

And then there are the actual skills you walk out of college with. For me, I got my degree in broadcast journalism. As you know, I didn't end up going into journalism—I took a hard left turn into ministry just a few months before I graduated. And for a while, I thought my degree was going to go to waste. But today, as an author, podcaster, and owner of a media company, I regularly use the skills I began to develop in college. Most of us do in one way or another—even if our major and career path aren't directly linked.

Our experiences also give us empathy for others who are experiencing the same thing. And the people we meet along the way—even if it's in a random French class we accidentally ended up taking in college—might end up changing our lives.

My point is that nothing is wasted. If you walk down a road, get to the end, and then have to completely retrace your steps, even that experience isn't a waste. You learned something along the way, you grew because of that journey, and that growth will serve you well in all kinds of ways down the road.

There's no one right way to do this, and if you make a

decision that you later feel was the wrong one, you can always do something different.

So, here's the plan: together, we're going to go through four steps to help you move closer to making a decision in any area of your life.

The steps are:

1. Gather your options
2. Clear the clutter
3. Turn doorknobs
4. Identify what you'll gain and give up

Gather Your Options

Before you decide what you're going to do, you need to figure out what you *could* do.

In the last chapter you looked outside yourself to fill your mind with possibilities, and looked inside to gain insight and clarity on what you truly want. Now it's time to write down your options.

We are still far from making a decision. You don't have to know what you want to do just yet. Right now you're just making a list of all the options before you.

In *The Life-Changing Magic of Tidying Up*,[2] organization expert Marie Kondo instructs people to gather similar items from all around their house before getting rid of any of them. Instead of making decisions drawer by drawer ("Do I want to keep this Chapstick? Yeah, I probably need it.") she wants you to go around your house and locate all the miscellaneous Chapsticks floating around in random drawers and purses. Then once you see how many you actually have, you can decide which ones to keep and where you want to store them.

This is the best way to cut down on unnecessary clutter, to clear mental and physical space and keep only the things that you use, need, or like. (Things that spark joy!)

The principle for this step is the same. Until you have all your options laid out in front of you, it's hard to focus on the decision you're trying to make. And if your mind is trying to hold all the variations and possibilities and pros and cons all at once, it will be too busy juggling those details to actually evaluate them.

So here's your first step. Get a piece of paper or a napkin, or open a blank document or spreadsheet on your computer— whatever method works for you—and get those details out of your head.

Be as specific as you can be. Recently Carl and I were trying to figure out childcare options for our girls (quite the task—the only reason we got into the preschool we ended up choosing was because it had just opened and we got in line at four in the morning!). On our spreadsheet, we included as much information as possible for each school—all the relevant variables. We wrote down the hours of the school, the proximity to our house, the type of teaching the girls would receive and how we felt about it, whether or not it was open in the summer, how much it cost, and anything else we could think of.

With all those key details out of our heads and where we could see them, we were able to compare them more easily: "Okay, this school is cheaper, but it's fifteen minutes farther away from our house. How much are those fifteen minutes worth? What will that fifteen minutes be like in rush hour traffic?"

As you're listing out all your options and starting to move them around and play with them— deleting some and amending others—you'll start to notice areas of your life where you're willing to be flexible, and areas where you're simply not. This is really helpful information. I call these your fixed elements and your variables.

FIXED ELEMENTS

Your fixed elements are decisions you've already made that you organize the rest of your life around, or things you know you want to be true about your life, so you use them as guiding principles when deciding anything else. They're your nonnegotiables.

When I got married, Carl became a fixed element in my life. Other elements can still change: we could get new jobs, or change houses or cities. Our hobbies might shift and our weekend commitments could be seasonal, but no matter what happens—wherever we move, whatever we do—we're going to do it together.

Spouses and kids aren't the only fixed elements in our lives—a fixed element can be almost anything you choose. A city or a specific house may be a fixed element in your life. Proximity to your family, living in the town where you grew up, living in the house your grandfather built—any of these could be a nonnegotiable, something you want to be true of your life even if everything else changes.

Deciding what our fixed elements are is powerful. It brings clarity, helping us know what to fight for and what we can let go of.

But it's important to examine our fixed elements—to pick them up and turn them over in our hands like a shell on the beach. Deciding that something's fixed when it doesn't have to be, or when it shouldn't be—that's one of the primary ways we get stuck.

My family and best friends live in Colorado, and they are wildly important to me. They are a fixed element in my life, so for years I was determined to move back to Colorado to be close to them. I was determined to do this even if it wasn't the best decision for my new husband, our marriage, or the careers we were working to build.

Thankfully, I took another look at my fixed element of moving home to Colorado—and I realized that Colorado itself wasn't a fixed element, but my people were. I crafted a work-around where Carl and I lived in another place (Nashville) but worked hard to set aside time and money so I could go home to Colorado as often as I wanted. I was there for baby showers and birthdays, graduations and just because. The path between Nashville and Colorado became so well-worn I really felt like I was living in both places. Sacrifices had to be made, but those sacrifices have been worth it. I would have sacrificed more if I had left Nashville, thinking that living in Colorado was the only way to be close to my people. It turns out it wasn't.

If you're going to structure your whole life around something, make sure that you choose it carefully—and that you're the one choosing it.

So, what are your fixed elements? Are they actually fixed, or have you just always thought they should be? What about them is fixed, exactly? And is the whole thing fixed, or can you prioritize what's at the heart of it and then get creative?

That's how motherhood is for me. My girls are fixed. Where I go, they go; where they go, I go. That's something I'll structure my whole life around. But what motherhood looks like exactly, that's variable. I know that I can be a good mom if I'm a stay-at-home mom, or if I'm working, or if I'm doing a little bit of both. I know I can be a good mom if we grow our own food in our backyard and also if we eat a few too many dino nuggets.

Pause for a moment and think through the fixed elements in your life. As you assess whether they're truly fixed, go back to the questions we asked in the "Get Free" chapter. Are your fixed elements fixed because you want them to be, or because you think they're supposed to be? Did someone tell you it had to be this way, and if so, is that a person you want guiding significant pieces of your life? Which fixed elements do *you* want to make your other life decisions around?

If anything comes to mind immediately, jot it down—maybe put it at the top of your page with a circle around it. That way you'll remember that you've already made a decision. This particular aspect of your life is a fixed element, so now you just need to decide what else goes around it.

VARIABLES

Your fixed elements are like the big pieces of furniture in your house. They're the investment pieces, heavy and expensive and hard to move. You want them to be high quality and long-lasting, and to work well for your lifestyle and your space—because they're just too big and clunky to swap in and out.

If the fixed elements in your life are the couch and the entertainment center, the variables are the throw pillows, the lamps, the end tables, the art, the rug, and the cozy blankets you switch up throughout the year.

The variables in your life are easier to change; you can move them around the fixed elements. They're important and powerful and can significantly impact your quality of life—they're just a little easier to shuffle around.

For some people, their job might be a variable—they change jobs periodically depending on their current financial, relational, and personal needs. They move their job around their life, not their life around their job.

For other people, a variable might be their home or city.

There's no one place that has to be their place, so while it does take some time and effort and yes, maybe a moving truck, their location is something they're willing to play with in order to improve their quality of life.

Smaller variables might be things like schedule or routine or hobbies or social commitments. You care about these things, and they significantly affect the way your life looks and feels, but they're things you can change and reimagine when you need to.

Once you've taken the time to write out your options and started to identify some of your fixed elements and variables, you can move to the next step in our decision-making process.

Clear the Clutter

Homes and the stuff inside them say a lot about the people who live there. But no matter how intentional we may be with what we bring into our homes, we often still end up with items that were chosen for us all over the house.

We're surrounded by mail that was sent to us, magazines we didn't subscribe to, and coupons we don't want but that are cluttering up our kitchen counters anyway. Maybe we own a piece of furniture that was purchased quickly to meet a specific need, but we don't actually like it. Or maybe we have a collection of hand-me-down pieces rescued from parents or friends or siblings. (Who doesn't love hand-me-downs?!) Our closets may be full of impulse buys, pieces of clothing that don't fit, accessories we've had since college, or well-intentioned gifts that just aren't our style.

If we aren't paying attention, this stuff grows to be part of the architecture of the house. We all have that random bowl that's been on our kitchen counter forever—the one holding a few lost pennies, a screw that goes to something but we're not sure what, a remote without batteries, and a piece of candy that's long since gone stale. Or that basket that's been sitting in the corner of our guest room for so long, we don't even see it anymore.

It's easy to collect; it's much harder to curate. It's hard to keep new things from entering our space, or to remove them once they're already there.

And this can be true of our lives as well as our homes.

So your next step is to clear the clutter. We're going to make space for the options that might fit into your life by eliminating the ones that don't. Eliminate the options and elements that don't serve you, that don't fit your vision for your life, or that you just know you don't want.

Saying a definitive no, even to just one thing, is empowering. It shows you that you can.

Saying no can be hard, but once you get started, it's also exhilarating, freeing, and empowering. You feel bold and strong and full of authority.

So that's our next step. Look over your list of options and find one that you're ready to say no to—one that you know just does not fit. If you're having a hard time, try adding an option to your list that you *know* you're going to say no to—something that's not even a question. (That's not cheating, it's just helping you get started!)

Sometimes the clearest way to see what you want is by looking for what you don't.

Turn Doorknobs

Now that you've gathered your options, identified your fixed elements and variables, and cleared out the clutter of the options you definitely aren't going to choose, it's time to take some action! But notice that you're going to take action before you make your final decision—and that's on purpose.

Have you ever lost sleep trying to decide between two things, only to find out that one of them wasn't even an option? I definitely have. We do this all the time.

Maybe you're looking for a new place to live. Whether you're looking to buy or looking to rent, you've certainly spent more than a few minutes scrolling through your favorite real estate app. You find an apartment you like—you think this might be the one. But just as you're about to reach out, you see another apartment you like just as much. Now you're stuck. They're both great, but they're great in different ways. One is bigger, newer, and significantly nicer, but those benefits come with a hefty price tag. The other is quite a bit smaller and older, and not quite as nice. But it's cheaper, and it's about ten minutes closer to work. Would you rather spend more and have more or spend less and get less? Are those ten minutes important to you? Do you want to be close to work? Or does the other apartment offer proximity to things you might enjoy even more than having a shorter commute?

Before you know it, you're stuck. You're weighing the pros and cons, maybe even making a spreadsheet with all the variables. You've sent the listings to several friends to get their input, and you've legitimately lost sleep as you've laid awake trying to picture your life in each of the apartments. You even know where your furniture would go in each of them, you just can't decide which one is a better fit.

You struggle for a few days before you finally flip a coin. You're going to go with the more expensive apartment—except that when you finally get a chance to speak with the landlord, you find out that the apartment's no longer available.

You hang up and quickly dial the number for the other apartment, only to find out that it's gone too. In fact, it had been rented the day before you first saw it—they just hadn't taken the listing down yet.

Hello . . . can I get those hours of my life back please?

It's incredibly frustrating to find out we've wasted time deliberating over options that turn out not to be options after all. And that's why at this point in the process, we're going to take some definitive steps forward.

This is principle number three: Start turning doorknobs. Open up as many doors as you can, any that you might consider maybe, possibly, an option. See what additional information you can gather by looking through the doors, and then you can decide which one to walk through.

What does this look like? It looks like finding an apartment you're interested in and reaching out right away to find out if it's still available. Find another one you like? Reach out about that one too. Maybe you apply for both apartments. If you get both, then you can choose between the two. If you get just one, you have your answer.

This is helpful when dating too. In my many conversations with women over the years, I've noticed that we often spend a lot of time talking to guys online but relatively little time actually going on dates. This ends up being such a waste of both time and emotional energy. Say you're trying to figure out if a guy you're chatting with would be a good fit for you. Until you actually meet him in person, you're trying to make that decision with about a quarter of the information you need. The information that will truly help you make the decision is only available to you once you go on a date, maybe two. After one date, you'll know if you want to see this guy again, and that's what you're looking to find out with date two as well.

All too often, we get stuck on the starting line because we're trying to make the perfect decision before we even have a decision to make.

So with as much mental discipline as you can muster, don't try to decide whether you're going to walk through a door until you find out if it will actually open. Don't spend time debating between two options until you know they're both available.

You can turn doorknobs to gather information about your options in many different areas of your life. You don't need to know if a guy is your future husband before you go on a lot (a *lot*!) of dates with him. You don't need to know which job you want to take before you've been offered either one. You don't need to decide whether you want to move until you take steps to figure out if it's a realistic option for you.

If you're considering buying a home, you can run the numbers to figure out how much you can afford. You can go through the mortgage application and preapproval process—that way if you find the right house, you're ready to make an offer. You can spend your Saturdays and Sundays wandering through open houses—making mental (or physical!) lists of your must-haves, nice-to-haves, and must-not haves in a house.

All those action steps help you walk a little further down the road, gaining clarity on the options available to you before it's time to decide.

And here's the beautiful thing: you can explore all the options with absolute freedom, because they're just that—options. You can start putting pieces into place for multiple versions of the Choose Your Own Adventure before you make your choice—and you can do so freely, knowing that just because you're ready to walk through a door, doesn't mean you have to. But also, walking through a door is much easier when you've done all the work and research and vetting already.

This process can be a beautiful way to prepare yourself to make your decision and then take the leap. And once you've made the decision, the hard part doesn't start then—you've already done it! The last thing you have to do is jump.

Identify What You'll Gain and Give Up

Now that you've figured out what your options actually are, it's time to pick one. So, the last tool I want to share with you is something that has helped me tremendously in deciding between two good things.

Making decisions involves finding the right balance between what you want to gain and what you're willing to give up. Every choice comes with a trade-off, and we're all working with limited space, time, energy, and resources. It's up to us to decide how to allocate them.

You've likely made a few pro and con lists over the years—in a journal, on a napkin, or even just in your head. For our last step, I propose a similar type of cost-benefit analysis—but with a few twists.

You're going to take a sheet of paper, as big as you need, and write the decision you're trying to make—the option you're considering—at the top. We're not comparing and contrasting at this point, so don't write, "Do I take Job A or Job B?" Just write, "Do I take Job A?" We're going to consider one option at a time with this method. Below that, divide the sheet into two columns. Label the left column "What I'll gain," and the right column "What I'll give up."

Now, brainstorm. Write down everything you can think of that you'd gain by making this decision—taking Job A in this case. It can be big stuff like "I'll finally be able to pay off my debt" or "I'll get to live near my family," or small stuff like "They have a good coffee shop in the building next door" or "The office has a great view"—both gains, for sure!

In the next column, write down everything you'd be giving up. Maybe Job A would be more stressful than your current position, so you'd be giving up some mental freedom. Maybe it's more time-consuming too; write that down. If you take the job, you won't get to work with your current coworkers anymore, and that would be a real loss, because they're amazing! Maybe the job requires more driving than you're used to. Write down everything you can think of that this decision is likely to cost you, take away from you, or require you to give up.

Once you're done, you're going to assign each item on both lists a number from one to three. Assign the number based on each item's importance to you, with three being the most important. (Picture the two columns on either side of a scale—we're trying to see which one's heavier.)

Maybe being able to pay off debt gets a full three. That's a huge deal for you and would be a game changer. So you give three points to the "gain" column for that item. Same for living near your family. That would be a dream come true for you. You'll give the "gain" side three for that as well. For the coffee shop next door, you give it a one. It's a perk, but not a deal maker or breaker. The view, on the other hand, gets a two. You'd love the chance to work in a space that feels beautiful and inspiring; that view would enhance your quality of life and allow you to appreciate the beauty of your city every day.

When you add up all those numbers, you get nine.

Now let's do the other side:

When it comes to Job A being more stressful than your current position, maybe you assign that a two. You know it'll be more stressful, but not majorly so. It'll be noticeable but not unbearable. For time-consuming, you give that a three. That's something you're worried about—you have a lot of freedom in your current position, so that would be a hard shift. Giving up your coworkers feels rough, but you know you'll still be able to stay in touch with them, so you give that a one. And the fact that you'll have to drive a little bit more with this position gets a one as well.

For this side, you total up your losses, and you're at a seven.

Now, this doesn't mean you automatically say yes to the job, but it does help give you a sense of the balance between what you'd be gaining and what you'd be giving up.

The traditional pros and cons list doesn't involve giving different items the weight they hold for you. That's why I love this method. It has helped me think more clearly about my options when I'm trying to make a decision.

In this example, you would repeat the two-column process for the other job you're considering, for staying at your current position, for quitting it all and moving into your parents' basement to work on your e-commerce business, etc. And at the end, you'd be able to see all your options laid out in front of you, with a personalized cost-benefit analysis for each.

There's one more thing to think about as you're weighing your options—and that's long-term gains. Every so often, a decision feels like a less-than-ideal one in the short term. It feels like we'll have to give up a lot if we choose that option. But when we look at the big picture of our lives and where we want to go overall, that option will help us get there.

My best friend Kelsey's story is an incredible example of this. Kelsey and her husband, Tyler, have two of the greatest little boys ever, and when they were born, Kelsey initially thought she was going to continue working. She loved her job. But the further she got into new motherhood, the more she realized that what she was giving up by working her job was substantial. She and her husband were paying for childcare while she worked, and the math wasn't overwhelmingly positive—they were paying almost as much as she was making. And her job was causing their family a lot of stress. It wasn't a traditional nine to five (it required her to be gone on lots of nights and weekends), and she felt like she was missing out on precious time with her baby and her husband. It felt like her family was barely hanging on by a thread with all the balls they were trying not to drop.

But here's the thing: she didn't want to pause her career. She loved her job, and she wanted to keep working. Actually, she wanted to go back to school and get her master's in counseling so she could be a therapist—but she knew that dream was on hold for the time being.

After doing a cost-benefit analysis, weighing what she and her family would be gaining if she stayed home for a season and what she'd be giving up in the short term by making that choice, Kelsey made the difficult and painful decision to quit her job and stay home full-time.

This wasn't what she wanted—or at least, it wasn't everything she wanted. In quitting her job, she was gaining more time with her boys and more sanity and peace for everyone involved. But she was also giving up a major part of herself, as well as signing up for a different hard job—24/7 caretaking.

They had a bigger-picture plan in mind, though. She was going to stay home until the boys got a little older, and then she'd start school so that once they were in school she could start a new career as a therapist. This was the option they figured would cost the least and yield the most gains—not just in the short term, but in the long term.

Kelsey going back to school with two little kiddos at home was also a hard decision, though. It was expensive, costing them both time and money. But this time the math came out differently; she could see that this investment in her education would pay off for the rest of her life.

Over the years, it's been such a gift to watch Kelsey and Tyler make decisions together. They've made decisions they were excited about, some they were not excited about, some that were high-gain and low-cost, and some that cost a lot but led to just the right gains for their family in a particular season. And along the way, they've raised two incredible little boys. They've set themselves up for success as a family, and they've made space for both of them to pursue their passions. They've shared the load of finances and family and who's going on the school field trip, and they've built an incredible life—a life that looks like them and works for them.

As you're approaching your own decisions, know that sometimes a decision that doesn't sound so great in the moment can end up bringing you more gains in the long term than what you'll have to give up in the short term. Those decisions can be incredibly uncomfortable and even painful. But at the end of the day, you'll be grateful that while you were making the decision, you weren't just thinking about your current self; you were thinking about your future self and your future family as well.

One last reminder before we move on: You're not looking for the perfect answer here. There *is* no perfect answer. All you're looking to do is find your next step—the next step *you* want to take toward the life *you* want to live. And remember: If you get a ways down your chosen path and realize it isn't the path you want to be on, you can always make a new decision. And that doesn't mean you'll lose all the progress you've made, either. You'll be able to keep all the growth, development, skills, and wisdom you've gained along the way—and you'll get to apply them in a new way on a new path. So as much as you can, take the pressure off. You're looking for a good next step. Not one bit of this has to be perfect.

PART THREE

PIVOTS AND

ROADBLOCKS

CHAPTER TEN

WHAT IF YOUR PEOPLE DISAGREE?

Okay, we have to pause here because if you're anything like me, you love the idea of living an authentic, creative life that fits you just right—but there's something holding you back from believing that this could be a reality. What if your people disagree with you—or worse, disapprove of you? Now that we've talked about how to make a decision that's all your own, we need to pause and recognize that there might be fallout because of the decision you made—and we need to talk about what to do with that.

First, let's just be honest. This is hard. There's a reason we follow the pack—it's easier. There's a reason we do what other people tell us to do—it's because their disapproval and disappointment hurts. It's one thing to have a stranger give you the side-eye in the grocery store (I don't even like when *that* happens!), but it's quite another to have a key person in your life disagree with a big decision you're making. What do we do then?

Defending Your Decisions

No matter how long we've been creating a life on our own terms and how intentionally we've done so, we're going to have moments when we feel criticized for our choices, or when an

135

innocent comment pokes at a place that still feels tender—an old decision we made, maybe one that was hard and that we still question sometimes.

Expectations—explicit, implicit, or assumed—still weigh on us, no matter how long or how intentionally we've tried to shake them.

This is all normal. It's hard, painful at times, but it's normal. And just because it happens, just because it bothers you, doesn't mean you're doing anything wrong.

There's no one right way to build a life. Everyone has different fixed elements and different variables to play with. Everyone has different needs and wants. This is even true for our closest people, friends or family who are similar to us in both personality and values. We still have different cards we're playing with.

Learning that our life decisions are not binary is a constant process. Rarely is there a clear, singular Correct Answer and an opposite Wrong Decision. We'll always be making decisions about our lives, and other people will always be making decisions about theirs, and there will always be moments when we choose differently from someone else and when we (or they!) feel tension as a result.

Finding ourselves in these moments isn't a problem, but how we handle those flashes of panic or shame matter deeply. There was a time in my life when I would have totally rethought a decision because of an offhand comment.

And there's a deep fear that still rattles around in my bones from time to time: "If my friend is doing it this way, am I wrong for doing it differently?" Often, I'll make a decision that involves me doing something I've never done before. These decisions tend to be made tentatively and with a question mark at the end: "I'll take option . . . A?" So when I see a friend who I deeply love and admire choosing a different door entirely, it shakes my confidence. It leaves me wondering if I'm doing something wrong because she chose something different.

But there's a quote I love to come back to in moments like these. It's from comedian Amy Poehler. In talking about childbirth, motherhood, and all the different ways a woman can choose to bring a small human into the world, she says, "Good for her! Not for me."[1]

Or, my slightly amended version: "I get to decide, and so does she."

Who Are You Willing to Disappoint?

One tool has helped me considerably when it comes to making unpopular decisions—or decisions I know some people in my life might not be thrilled about. I ask myself, where do these people fall on my list? If I had to make a list of the people who are most important to me, who I'm the most responsible to and responsible for, where do these people rank?

The idea of ranking your people sounds cruel, doesn't it? But it's been such a helpful tool for me, because without it, I find myself trying to please everyone, and disappointing everyone in the process. For most of my life, my nuclear family—my mom, my dad, and my sister—was at the top of my list, and rightly so. But then something happened—I got married and had kids of my own. While that didn't demote my family of origin, it did carve out some new spaces above them.

My daughters come before my mom, for example. They

have to. I'm more responsible to and for my daughters than I am for my mom. My mom is *very* high up on my list. But if I'm forced to choose, I have to choose my daughters. (Part of that is because my mom has the ability to care for herself and my daughters do not!)

Responding to Those Who Disagree

So, that brings us back to the question of what you should do with pushback. What do you do when people don't agree with you?

It's up to you, and it depends on who it is.

Some people do not need an explanation. A great-uncle you've met twice, someone you went to high school with but haven't seen since, a stranger on the internet—these people's words may affect you (they always do for me), but you don't owe them an explanation. If they want to be in a tizzy about a decision you're making, that's their burden to carry—not yours.

Other people merit a conversation. You can offer an explanation to those you are close with and care about. You can take the time to hear their perspective. You're under no obligation to do anything differently because of that conversation if you don't want to. But if you want to have the conversation, you can.

Depending on who the person is, how high they are on your list, and the decision in question, you may decide to do something different based on their perspective—if you want to. You can make some concessions or compromises, or see if you can find a work-around.

But ultimately, at the end of the day, you're not responsible for their life, and you're not responsible for what they think of your life. You're responsible for you.

What If Your Decision Hurts Someone Else?

But what if your decision doesn't just impact you—what if it impacts someone else? And even harder, what happens when what's best for us hurts someone else—someone we deeply love?

Many of us have been conditioned to be people pleasers, to do whatever we can to make others happy. That seems like the loving thing to do, and above all else, we should be loving—right?

But here's an important truth: what feels loving in the short term might not actually be loving in the long term. What causes pain in the short term might prevent more significant pain in the long term.

I think about friends who've gone through painful breakups that surprised and disappointed people in their lives—especially their former partners. Staying in those relationships would have saved tons of pain in the short term. But how much pain does it cause to stay in a relationship that you know deep down isn't right? Lying to yourself and someone you love—stuffing down the realization you know to be true—it's excruciating.

And what about the long term? Is it loving to stay in a relationship for a decade to avoid hurting a partner? Is it loving to make them miss out on the full life they could have lived with someone else if given the chance? And how much more painful would it be for a jilted partner to have their relationship end ten, twenty, thirty years from now—or to still be together but find out that their partner hasn't been fully in it the way they thought they were?

These aren't easy questions to answer. Philosophers have spent their lifetimes debating the ends and the means and which justifies the other.

But when it comes to your life, these questions aren't anyone's to answer but yours.

This brings us back to a question we asked earlier in the book: What decision can you live with, and what decision do you want to live with?

And remember: If someone disagrees with your decision, the way they choose to react is a reflection of them, not you. If a person is truly on your side, they will support and love you even if they don't fully understand why you've made certain choices for your life.

CHAPTER ELEVEN

MAKING DECISIONS TOGETHER

I like to compare marriage to running a three-legged race.

When you first get married, you tie your legs together, and at first it feels fun. It's silly, and you laugh as you take your first wobbly three-legged steps together. Right, then left, wait, that doesn't work. Outside leg or inside leg?

But then someone yells "Go!" and you're off. You're moving at a much faster pace now, and this is when it starts to get hard. You try to take charge at the exact same moment your partner does. "Outside leg!" you shout, right as he yells, "Inside!" And because your legs are tied together, this probably lands you in a heap.

"Let's try this again," you might say as you awkwardly attempt to stand up together, wondering, just for a second, if this was such a fun idea after all.

The tricky thing about three-legged races is how they force you to work together. You can't accomplish your goal if you and your partner aren't communicating and working as a team. You have to talk to each other, coordinating every step. You have to agree.

You also have to move at the same pace. You can't rush ahead even if you feel like the other person is slowing you down.

When Carl and I first got engaged, so many couples told us, "Marriage is hard." They'd drop that discouraging insight and then shake their heads and walk away like they were reliving memories of arguments past.

These words always confused me. What did they mean? Hard *how*? Like, hard but worth it? Or hard and definitely not worth it? Were these couples recommending that we break off our engagement? Or should we still get married but seriously lower our expectations of what marriage would be like? What were we supposed to do with this information?

I always found this advice to be vague and unhelpful and also wildly discouraging, so when Carl and I got married, one of the first things I did was look around to try to figure out what all those married couples had been talking about.

Now, I fundamentally disagree with the idea that marriage is one-size-fits-all hard. Challenges are different for every couple because every couple is unique and so are their circumstances.

But there is one difficulty that every marriage I've ever seen has in common, and a three-legged-race is the best way I've found to explain it.

When you get married, you're basically tying your legs together—committing to share your finances, your home, and even your bed. It's intimate stuff! And now, both rookies at being tied to another person, you're off. You're charged with the task of tackling life together.

Sometimes this is easy, and often it's fun. But there's also an inherent awkwardness as you're figuring out how to work together. There are about a thousand things to trip over, and opportunities to bump into each other and hurt each other's feelings. You have two people's bills and debt and finances to manage. You have two people's belongings to shove into a closet that didn't magically get bigger when you got married. You have two people's daily habits and preferences, and you have two people with differing hopes and dreams and frustrations and bad moods—it's a lot to manage.

And if all that isn't tricky enough, sometimes life turns up the heat even more.

Before our first anniversary, Carl and I had been through the cancer diagnosis of one of our closest family members. Then, we lost another family member in a tragic, unexpected way. We lost two jobs each, moved to a new city, started two new businesses, and bought a house. There were few major life upheavals we hadn't experienced—and that was just in the first year.

Suddenly you're not just walking with your legs tied together, navigating the awkwardness of coordinating your steps. Now you're running, leaping over obstacles, ducking, dodging, and rolling, and trying to do it all as one unit.

Now, marriage itself can be hard, absolutely. But the simple truth is that *life* is hard, and when you're married, you have to figure out how to navigate it all as a team.

In this chapter, we're going to talk about what happens, or what happened in my life, rather, when I was no longer the only decision-maker. Things get a little more complicated when creating a life you love becomes a group project.

We're going to talk about how to build a life you love when your definition of a good life isn't the only one that matters anymore. How do you create a life that you love together?

———

Carl and I were standing in my apartment, making pasta for dinner and talking about the future. Our wedding was in just three and a half months, and in between addressing invitations and talking with the florist and scheduling dress and tux fittings, we were trying to piece together the other parts of our rapidly approaching future. Where did we want to live? What did we want to do for work? Who did we want in our community as we established ourselves in our brand-new marriage?

We had spent the last year working together in the marketing department at the nonprofit where we met. We had rhythms and friends and mentors and a life here together in this little town in north Georgia. We loved it, but we also knew that we wouldn't be there forever. The town was small and far away from both of our families, and while our jobs were great, we both knew that eventually we wanted to strike out on our own.

Carl wanted to start his own branding agency and I wanted to be an author. We knew that at some point, those dreams would take us somewhere new—but not yet. So much was about to change as we got married and blended our lives together, we thought it was wise to keep everything else as steady and stable as possible.

"One transition at a time," Carl said, and I nodded, resolutely.

Two weeks later, we were laid off.

Both of us. We both lost our jobs three months before our wedding.

Carl came in late on the morning of the reaping (as we started calling it). I came into work like it was any other day. I chatted with my coworkers, I sipped my coffee, I responded to a few emails, but then I noticed that one by one, my coworkers were being called in to meet with our boss, and they weren't coming back.

"That's weird," I thought, and then went back to my emails.

A few minutes later, our boss called my name.

The meeting was a blur. "It's not your fault. You did nothing wrong. The company needs to cut back on expenses. We're having to lay off so many people." None of these words made me feel any better.

He handed me an envelope with a severance check in it—a few weeks of pay to help me transition to the next thing—and then said I should clean out my desk immediately.

Wait, immediately? No two weeks? No transition? Don't I need to give my passwords to someone, teach someone else how to do my job?

Nope, effective immediately.

I took my envelope and started for the door in a daze. I never thought anything like this would happen to me.

That's when it hit me. "What about Carl?" I turned back. "Wait, what about Carl? Does he still have a job?"

My former boss shook his head like he was shaking off the question: "No, Steph, I have to be the one to talk to him." But that was all I needed to hear. Carl was losing his job too.

Carl arrived at the office a few minutes later, and before long, he emerged onto the patio where I was waiting. He had an envelope too.

We walked toward each other and into a tight hug. "We're going to be okay. We'll figure it out," Carl whispered into my hair.

We went back inside and cleaned out our desks. One by one, I put pictures and hard drives and loose papers into a box— packing up the pieces of a life I wanted to keep living. Out of the corner of my eye, I could see Carl doing the same thing. This chapter was over. What in the world were we going to do next?

The next three months felt like we were on a competition show for newly engaged couples. "Here, you've barely figured out how to work as a team—now complete this obstacle course together!" It was the most challenging (and most helpful, in hindsight) prewedding team-building activity I never could have imagined.

We had to figure out where to live, what to do for work, and how we were going to pay our bills. And we had to do all of that while still planning our upcoming wedding. We had stacks of papers on the dining room table in my apartment. There was a map of the Atlanta metro area, the floor plan of an apartment in Denver, the cover letter I'd been working on, and pieces of the design portfolio Carl was trying to put together.

On top of all that was our wedding RSVP list, and the itinerary for the wedding weekend, and the ceremony programs that Carl had just finished designing.

It felt like we were piecing together our entire life all at the same time, and this time, we didn't have any fixed elements.

Not only were we navigating all these logistics together, we were also going through the same thing at the same time but grieving it very differently. We were battered and bruised and deeply hurt. We hadn't just lost our jobs, we'd lost jobs we loved in a community we loved, in a town we loved but only lived in because of those jobs—there wasn't much of a reason to stay without them. We'd lost mentors we loved—we'd actually just been fired by them, if we're getting technical about it.

In the aftermath, I wanted to slow down. I wanted to rest, to hide away. I wanted space and time to process what had just happened and to heal from it. Carl wanted to move on, to move forward. He was sad and angry and hurt, of course. But he didn't want to spend time sitting in those feelings. He wanted to figure out what was next.

We worked hard to speak each other's language, to understand each other's needs and meet them, and for the most part, we were successful. But there were still times when he felt like I was dragging him down, or when I felt like he was rushing me forward.

We had to figure out what to do next, and we had to do it together. It felt like we were sitting in front of a twelve-thousand-piece puzzle without any corner or edge pieces.

So, we did what any rational people would do, I guess, and we got out a big piece of paper. We didn't have any fixed elements anymore, but if we had any hope of moving forward, we were going to need to decide on some.

Finding Our Fixed Elements

"Okay, in an ideal world, where would you want to live next?" Carl prompted, his pen hovering above the paper.

Truthfully? I wanted to go home to Denver. I was feeling tender, rejected, and betrayed after what we'd just gone through. I wanted to tuck my tail between my legs and go hide in my childhood bedroom for a while.

Carl wasn't quite as excited about that idea. *Oh, riiight, we have to find an option we both want*, I realized. I was so used to being in the driver's seat of my life, it was jarring to have a co-captain.

"Okay, let's start wide," he began again. "Let's make a list of all the places we could see ourselves living."

We started with Atlanta; it was the closest, after all. Then came Denver, where I grew up and where my family and best friends still live. Then came Indianapolis, where Carl grew up and where his family still lives. Then, we started listing places we'd been to and liked or hadn't been but thought we might like.

We were using the "throw spaghetti at the wall and see what sticks" approach—getting all our potential options out of our heads and onto the page.

Other than my instinct to run and hide, we didn't have a

north star. We didn't know what we wanted or where to look for it. The only fixed element we had was each other. Where we lived, how we lived, what we did for work—it was all up in the air.

We needed a filter of some kind. We needed to figure out what was important to us if we wanted to have any chance of getting it. We couldn't move forward until we had a direction.

As we brainstormed different places we could live, some themes emerged. What we wanted became clearer as we identified what we didn't—we were able to start clearing some clutter.

We want to live in a city, right? Yes. We're definitely not country people. *Okay, cities it is.*

We didn't want to be in a huge city—a medium-ish city felt more manageable. We wanted to be near family and friends, if at all possible. And we wanted to be able to do work we love, which meant being in a city with a thriving creative scene. A picture of what we were looking for was developing slowly, like a polaroid. We also wanted to keep our cost of living as low as possible. We wanted the freedom to do work we cared about, even if it didn't pay much at first, and we knew that wouldn't be an option in more expensive places.

We ended up with a list of medium-sized cities: Portland, Austin, Nashville, Charleston, Denver, Indianapolis—and then we added Atlanta and New York, breaking with our medium-city criteria because they checked other important boxes.

None of the options had everything we were looking for, but they all had a lot to offer. So, with our list in hand, we started our job searches. We applied to anything and everything we could find. We pursued hundreds of different opportunities, turning hundreds of doorknobs. We got canned responses from some companies, but in most cases we heard nothing. It was so discouraging, and it got progressively scarier as we got closer and closer to our wedding day with no idea how we were going to keep ourselves afloat. Then finally, a door cracked open. It was a part-time job for me as a writing assistant in Nashville. It wasn't perfect. It wasn't exactly what we were looking for. We still didn't know what Carl was going to do, and this part-time job wasn't going to fully support us (not even close). But it was a start, and it was the only start we had.

Carl could find a job in his line of work pretty much anywhere, he reasoned, and a step forward for one of us was a step forward for both of us. Nashville it would be!

Here's something I learned in this process: Even when you choose something good, it's not always easy. I was an active participant in our choice to move to Nashville. It was the best option—in a lot of ways, it was the only option. And it was a good one. A great one, actually. Anytime someone hears that we live in Nashville, they say, "Oh I *love* Nashville" or "I've *always* wanted to go there." But for the longest time, I didn't share their affection for the city.

It wasn't the city itself, although for a while, I wasn't quite sure where I fit there. It was more that we went from being surrounded by all kinds of people our age, in our same stage of life, to knowing absolutely nobody.

We had also just gotten married—so it was transition upon transition upon transition. New job, new city, new marriage, no friends to speak of . . . we were going through so many changes at the exact same time. I cried most days that first year, and my tears had very little to do with marriage itself being hard. *Life* was hard—even though I was pretty sure we'd made the right decisions.

That's the thing I learned that year. Even good decisions sometimes take a while to actually *feel* good. They take time, effort, grit, showing up every day and putting in the work—long after it feels good to do so.

But what happens on the other side of that perseverance, grit, and determination is something beautiful. We've lived in Nashville for almost ten years now, and it's been a wonderful home for us.

So, a little encouragement just in case you need it: don't judge a decision by how it feels right after you've made it. You might need to sleep on it, let some roots grow, see it in all different lights, and tend to it for a while. If you judge it right at the beginning, you're going to be seeing it through the eyes of someone who's tired, someone who's in the middle of a tough transition, and someone who really just needs a hug and a good meal. Give her some time. She'll get there.

What Can You Take Away?

I'm so glad I had the four steps I shared with you in the Get Moving chapter in my back pocket when Carl and I were going through all of this. I'm not sure how we would have moved forward without them. When you're making decisions with another person, it's especially helpful to have a clearly defined method to follow. Gathering your options is a great place to start. Get them out of your heads and onto the page so you can move them around, think through them, and identify which are your fixed elements—instead of spending all your mental energy keeping the options straight. Clearing the clutter is the next step—you may be able to look over your options and quickly see a few things you're sure you don't want. For Carl and me, saying "no" to those things was not only clarifying, it was empowering. It helped us feel—even if just for a moment—like we really could figure this out, and, even better, we could figure it out together. Next, start turning doorknobs. There's no sense in weighing the pros and cons of options that may not actually be options. So get to work making phone calls, sending emails, or doing whatever else you need to do to evaluate which options are available and realistic. Once Carl and I had our actual options on the table in front of us (or really, our lack thereof in this case), it was much easier to move forward. We didn't really even have to weigh what we were going to be gaining and giving up, because we really only had one viable option. Depending on your situation, you may have a handful of options to evaluate based on what you'd be gaining and giving up with each one—but once that's done, you'll have a much clearer sense of what your real options are, and that will help you make the final decision together.

In the next chapter, we'll talk much more about how to create a life you love together, a life you *both* love. And we'll start by talking about what happens when you're not on the same page.

CHAPTER TWELVE

WHAT TO DO IF YOU DON'T AGREE

Moving to Nashville wasn't easy, but it was a decision we made together without much conflict. (It's easier to make a decision together when you only have one option!)

When we arrived in Nashville, I started my part-time writing assistant job, and my boss's husband ended up offering Carl a job at the marketing company he was working to start. It was a total dream. Carl and I were both doing creative work with people we admired, and we got to do it together—both working in the same little office space that our bosses shared.

It felt like we were starting to build something good—a friend group (our bosses generously adopted us into theirs!), a life in Nashville, and work we liked. But then one day, it all fell apart. One minute Carl and I both had jobs, then over the course of an unexpected lunch and a perplexing "It's not you, it's me" conversation, our jobs were gone. It was over.

I felt totally betrayed, and I was angrier than I'd ever been before—my anger about this situation piling on top of still-fresh fury about the last time someone had said, "You're welcome here, we value you, make yourself at home, we'll take care of you," and then suddenly changed their mind.

On a cold January day, Carl and I cleaned out our desks, together, again—our only sources of income disappearing for the second time in a year. Four jobs lost before our first anniversary.

We were newlyweds in a new city—in the midst of the biggest transition of our lives so far—and we had no income, very few friends, and no clue where we were going to go from here. We were back to the drawing board, and this time we were *not* on the same page about how to move forward.

Should we go through the whole job-hunt circus again, applying for hundreds of jobs only to not hear back from any of them? Or, because we just couldn't seem to stay in the nests we kept trying to build for ourselves, was this our moment to fly?

Twice now, we'd learned that working for someone else isn't always a safe bet. And so, years ahead of when we thought we'd take this leap, we wondered if maybe now was the time to try working for ourselves. Carl wanted to start his own branding agency. I wanted to be an author. Was this the time to pursue these dreams? Or was this the time to buckle down, get serious, and get "real jobs"—something that could support our little family?

The other thing we had to figure out was where we wanted to live. We'd moved to Nashville for a job I no longer had. We didn't have pets, kids, or even houseplants. We still barely knew anyone else in town, we hadn't put down roots, and our lease was ending soon. If we could go anywhere, why would we stay here?

With a cocktail of anger, fear, and "You can't come to my birthday party" energy surging within me, I wanted to call Nashville a loss, pack my bags, and go somewhere far away.

It wasn't a bad idea, I reasoned. Carl and I met because we'd both backpacked around the world for a year. That was the foundation, in many ways, of our love story. We could easily do it again. I knew that we could find good Wi-Fi (almost!) anywhere, we could most likely find or create some sort of remote job, and the cost of living would be significantly less, say, in a little town we both loved on the coast of Cambodia, than it would be any-where stateside.

Let's *go*. That was my vote.

Carl, on the other hand, had been watching the housing mar-ket in Nashville. He knew that we'd want to buy a house at some point, and he had a feeling that if we didn't get into the market now, we'd have a much harder time doing it later. (Turns out he was right!)

Our legs were tied together, but we wanted to run in opposite directions. I wanted to sell all our stuff and leave the country; Carl wanted to stay and invest in our work and in a house. He thought that was the smart thing to do, the responsible thing. Suffice it to say, we weren't on the same page. Thus began one of the longest and trickiest conflicts in our marriage—one that took years to overcome.

The lowest point was Valentine's Day that year. We had no money, so we made dinner at home, turned the lights down low, and lit some candles. Ta-da, romance! As we ate, we talked about life, and I started to dream out loud:

"You know what I'd love to do someday, is move to Spain for a while. . . ."

I was picturing a year abroad, or maybe a hybrid option—we could spend a few months in the US, a few in Spain, and go back and forth. It was a far-off dream, a point on the horizon I thought we could consider pointing ourselves toward. It was essentially the grown-up version of making a hundred-item Christmas list in March. Sure, you're reaching, but it's fun to dream.

Carl, however, was not having fun. To him, my dreams felt like an expensive, complicated, insanely stressful order demanded from an already maxed-out kitchen staff.

He wasn't thinking about something fun we could do in the

future. He wasn't thinking about creative, beautiful, idealistic ways to spend our days. He was trying to figure out how we were going to pay for health insurance next month. He was trying to figure out what we were both going to do for work.

Carl snapped. "Stephanie, that's so unrealistic. That's not a thing people do. That's not real life." He was mad, and so he pushed back even harder:

"Also—Steph, what if I don't like Spain? What if I don't want to go to Spain? What if I never want to go to Spain? What then?"

He was angry and also feeling unheard, as if the dreams I had for my life and for our lives together were swallowing up his dreams. He felt like I was totally ignoring his needs. As I talked about jetting off to Spain, he heard the message that he was alone in our life today. He was the only one who realized there was only eleven dollars in our bank account, the only one who was going to show up to fix it.

So he leaned in to the responsibility angle. "Steph, we can't just 'move to Spain.' We have to get jobs, earn money, pay our bills, support our family. That's how this goes. That's what being a responsible adult looks like."

"But that's not life-giving, that's not fun, that's not what I want to do. I don't want to work long hours every single day at a job I hate in order to pay for a life I don't actually want," I countered—my eyes still on the big picture of our lives, not on our current predicament.

"That's adult life. Welcome!" he shot back angrily, and also extremely confidently. So confidently, it took me aback. Was he right? Were my dreams silly, unrealistic, irresponsible? Was I just now waking up to the truth that you can't actually build a life you love?

I was also realizing for the first time that because I had

married this person, I was now beholden to their dreams, desires, and needs as well as my own. And not only did I have to consider them, but I might need to sacrifice things that were important to me if they turned out to be incompatible with things that were important to him.

Incompatible.

I couldn't stop thinking about that word. I'd never thought about it before—not in relation to Carl, at least. He was my person. We were such a good fit. Our lives clicked together in so many ways. I thought we wanted the same things in life—but maybe we didn't. Maybe to be compatible with each other, we'd each have to lose part of ourselves. I was okay with some sacrifices, but resigning myself to a job I didn't want to pay for a life I didn't want in a place I didn't want to be—that felt like sacrificing everything.

Now, let me say, when Carl and I fight, we typically get through it quickly. We're both pretty good communicators, pretty good listeners, pretty good at conflict resolution. But this time was different.

After that night, every time I'd dare to bring up the subject of traveling, leaving, creating a new life, the fight would start all over again. We'd whip out our boxing gloves and back into our opposing corners—Carl getting more rigid and responsible and "*This is just the way things are. This is what responsible adults do*" with each round, and me backing further into the corner of "*People should get to love their lives, and to hell with responsibility, and it's a totally reasonable life choice to live out of a backpack for the rest of our lives.*" The more rounds we went, the more we became people we never wanted to be, fighting for things we didn't even want.

But because each of us felt the other one pulling back, we

pulled harder. We put more and more of our weight into pulling the other one toward our side, which led to our positions becoming more and more extreme.

"I don't care about travel; I don't care about loving our life. All I care about is setting ourselves up for retirement and paying our bills—and I don't think it's realistic to expect to love your job or your life anyway. Those are the fantasies of a privileged child. It's time to grow up."

That's what I heard him saying to me.

And what he heard me saying was,

"I don't care about our financial lives; I don't care about our future. I'm not interested in working or contributing to our family's stability, safety, or well-being, so it's all on you. I don't want a home or roots or community—I want to leave it all behind, and I don't care what you want."

What we finally realized was that neither of the things we were hearing was what the other person was actually saying.

A few years into this stalemate, I was talking on the phone with my best friend, Kelsey. She fills several seats in my cabinet—and this time, she saved the day as chief diplomat.

"Can you believe him? What is even happening? Who did I marry? How is it possible that we want such different things for our lives?" I raged into the phone.

"Steph," she responded, "Carl is a good person, a rational person, and a person who wants the same things out of life that you do. Walk me through this again. I feel like something's getting lost in translation here."

I told her about our predicament and about his rigidity (and I may have slightly downplayed mine). I told her about our boxing gloves and how much joy this conflict was stealing from us. I told her I wasn't sure we'd ever be able to get on the same page. It felt like the lives we wanted were mutually exclusive. I didn't know how we were going to move forward.

She asked good questions and listened to my answers and finally came to her conclusion. "Steph, I think you're both scared. I think you both want to be in the middle here, but you've pulled hard into your corners because you're afraid the other person is pulling hard in the opposite direction. I wonder what would happen if Carl knew you were on his team—if he knew you cared about the things he cares about. I wonder if that would free him to care about the things you care about—or to show you that he always has."

She was right. I never meant for my stance to get so extreme. I didn't actually want to be a nomad. I love having a home and a community; I wanted to have roots. I also cared about our financial lives; I wanted to be wise with our money and set ourselves up well, both in the present and for the future. I also *wanted* to work. I've always wanted to work. I was just hoping to find work I cared about and enjoyed, if that was at all possible. And last but not least, I cared about having a family and taking care of our family, and I knew that would need to include having insurance, paying our taxes, and saving for retirement—you know, adulty things.

It turns out, Carl's the same way. He loves to travel. He's creative and imaginative and deeply values new experiences. He's also not at *all* a "we do this because this is the way things have always been done" kind of guy. If anything, he's the opposite. He's a question asker, an innovator, and, occasionally, a bit of a rule breaker. He has big dreams for his life and for our life together, but he also felt a great responsibility to take care of the little family we were beginning to build for ourselves (he still does). Making sure our family is taken care of is incredibly important to him, and if I wasn't going to participate in that part of the plan, he felt it would have to become his entire focus and responsibility.

We'd become so polarized, but neither of us actually wanted the thing the other person thought we did. We each had to start validating and supporting the other person's needs and desires before they would be able to do that for us. Carl needed to know that I cared about taking care of our family before he could let himself dream. He couldn't get lost in a far-off fantasy about moving to Spain when he knew we only had eleven dollars in our bank account. He needed a foundation before we could fly. My job became getting on his team, or rather, showing him that I'd been there all along. I had to creep over to his side of the ring, trusting that once we got a few things in place, he'd creep back toward mine.

And he did. The more I started fighting for his cause, the more he was able to fight for mine—and vice versa. It was like a dance. I became more proactive about our finances and life logistics, which freed Carl up enough to start dreaming for our family, and we got closer and closer to standing together in the middle—which is exactly where we'd both wanted to be all along.

Now we just had to figure out what to do next.

During one of our most memorable conversations on the subject, Carl told me about rookies getting drafted into the NFL: "They're so excited to be drafted, and they're picturing a long and profitable career in football. So when they're given a signing bonus—which is more money than most people in their early twenties have ever had—they blow it. They buy a car, they buy jewelry, they travel, they treat their friends. The problem is, most NFL careers last about two years. Some of these guys may not make it through training camp. They may not make the team.

So when they spend that piece of early success, they quickly find themselves back at square one with nothing.

"Steph, I know you want to leave, but I think if we stay here, go all in on our work, buy a house, and invest some of the flexibility we have right now instead of spending it, we'll be able to use it later in a longer-term more sustainable way—instead of using all our freedom up front and having to start over when we get back."

His point made sense. I was so tired of square one.

The housing market in Nashville was starting to heat up, but mortgages were still cheaper than paying rent. Carl was sure this was our moment to jump into homeownership—he thought we'd regret it if we didn't. He thought we'd be able to build our businesses more easily if we were in one place, with a desk and reliable Wi-Fi—and still in the same time zone as the people we were trying to work with.

So that's what we did. We were already in Nashville, so that's where we decided to stay for a while. We bought a little house in an up-and-coming area. We got better insurance, and we started saving for retirement. And we poured all our time, energy, and love into our little businesses.

I didn't love everything about our life back then. I did love some parts of it, absolutely, but not all of it. We weren't exactly living my dream life as we hustled and saved and paid off debt and let our passports gather dust for a while. But we were building the foundation for the life I wanted in the long term.

What Does It Mean for You?

As you're reading this, maybe you're single or in a new relationship, hopeful about the future but waiting to see where the relationship is headed. You're the primary decision-maker in your life; it's not a group project at the moment. The story I just shared is one I wish I could go back and tell myself when I was single, because I think it would have provided some helpful insight. First of all, I would have been relieved to hear this description of marriage—that marriage is hard in the way all relationships are hard, but also that it's hard because you're two people driving one car. Of course that's hard. That totally makes sense. I would have been relieved to hear that there wasn't some sort of unimaginable marriage secret waiting for me at the end of the aisle. I would have gotten a better idea of what to expect from marriage and how to prepare for it.

Speaking of preparing for marriage, one of the best things you can do while you're single is to figure out who you are, what you want, and where you want to go. Knowing all of this will help tremendously as you're deciding whether or not to tie your life to someone. It's hard to know if you'll be compatible race partners if you don't have a clue where you're each headed.

I've also been telling single women for years that the healthier they can become while they're single, the healthier their marriage will be. Self-reflection and growth is work that you can start right now—healing from the past, working through the places where you consistently get stuck, and building the skills that will help you when it's time to be in a relationship.

The more healing and growing you do ahead of time, the less baggage you'll have to schlep into your relationship and the better equipped you'll be to handle the hard moments that come along.

Another thing Carl and I tell couples all the time is that when a prospective partner tells you (or shows you) who they are and what they want in life, you need to believe them. Don't marry them hoping or believing that one day they'll change their mind or become someone else. If they say they don't want kids, or only want to live in a city, or want to work a job that requires lots of travel, or if they really don't like to travel and don't think they ever will—listen to them. You're not just choosing a romantic partner, you're choosing a co-captain. What they want matters, because it might be what you end up with. Attaching yourself to someone who wants to head west when you have your heart set on going east is going to leave both of you frustrated and potentially disappointed with the way your life turns out. You can compromise, absolutely. But make sure that the relationship isn't going to cost you the things that are most important to you—the things that make you *you*.

Even if you marry someone who's on the same page as you in many ways, you'll inevitably have times when you don't see eye to eye, just as Carl and I did. Since that's going to happen regardless, it's helpful if you *do* see eye to eye on as many important things as possible. So make sure to have in-depth conversations about your hopes, dreams, values, goals, the things you want in life, and what it looks like to go after them. Make sure you have them *before* you get married. Before you tie your leg to someone else's, make sure you're headed in the same direction.

But maybe you're not single right now. Maybe you're engaged or newly married, or you've been married for years, and you're experiencing firsthand the truth that while creating a life you love is hard, creating a life you both love is even harder. Group projects are notoriously difficult and frustrating, and this one is no different.

After experiencing this truth in our own lives, Carl and I have several things we often advise other couples to do when they find themselves similarly stuck.

Ask for Help

I wish we would have asked for help sooner. We'll talk about this more in the next chapter, but asking for help isn't a sign of weakness, it's a sign of strength.

I wish we would have invited our cabinet into our conflict sooner—but the good news is that you don't have to wait as long as we did. If you find yourself stuck in a place you just cannot seem to get out of, or if you find yourself at an impasse in your relationship, or if there's an issue you seem to get tripped up by over and over again, ask for help. Ask a friend, mentor, or therapist to weigh in. There is no shame in asking for help, and there is so much freedom and clarity to be gained when you do.

Trade Off

When two people are making decisions together, there has to be give and take. Carl and I had our first chance to practice this when we moved to Nashville, and we've had a thousand chances since. Sometimes an option or opportunity will be equally good for both of us, but we've found that this is rarely the case. Usually, an option is a great fit for one of us, and fine for the other, and we've leaned into this over the years. We've worked to practice the truth that a step forward for one of us is a step forward for both of us. That's true for your relationship too. A raise, a promotion, an opportunity, or an open door for one of you, is actually good for both of you—because you're a team. You're tied together, remember?

When an opportunity comes up for either Carl or me, one of the ways we evaluate it is by seeing if the other can help make it work without sacrificing everything. Here's an example.

Several years ago Carl looked into going to grad school. Most of the schools he was considering were in the Boston area, which meant I could have suddenly found myself a resident of New England—a place I'd never lived before.

Were there opportunities for me in Boston? Probably! It's an awesome city. I would have found a place for myself there. But we would have been going to Boston for him, not for me. It would have been great for him, and fine for me. And it really would have been fine. I can bring my work anywhere; that's one of the reasons I chose the career path that I did. I wanted as much flexibility as possible, and I truly have it. So if Carl's dreams brought us up to Boston, I could have easily gone without sacrificing mine.

But it's important that both partners get opportunities to take big steps forward—instead of one being dragged along all the time.

We moved to Nashville for my career, not his. We moved so I could take the part-time writing assistant job. But we also moved because Nashville is such a creative city, packed full of incredible authors, podcasters, small business owners, and creators. We figured it would be the perfect place to live while I tried to enter that creative world.

When we made the decision, Carl was doing some freelance design work, and he could have done that anywhere. But we knew that a step forward for one of us was a step forward for both of us, so we took the step to Nashville for me.

After we lost our first jobs in Nashville, I was ready to move on—to slam the door on Nashville—but Carl wasn't. It turned out that Nashville wasn't just a great fit for me; it was a great fit for him too. It was the perfect launching pad for his dream, the branding agency he'd always wanted to build, and so we stayed.

I wanted to go, but we stayed. It was his turn to take a step forward, so even though that step kept us right where we were, we took it for him.

If you're going to create a life you love, a life you *both* love, there are going to be some trade-offs. And you might end up taking turns. You might find an opportunity that launches one of you forward and that the other person can live with, and then, the next time, the roles might be reversed. It's worked for us, and I believe it can for you as well.

Think about Short Term vs. Long Term

There's one more thing we talk to couples about when they find themselves in moments of conflict or confusion. As you're creating a life you both love, and doing it together, you have to find a balance between decisions that offer short-term benefits and ones that will pay off more in the long term.

Carl and I have decided that we're not willing to completely sacrifice the short term for the long term, or vice versa. We want to sacrifice some of both for the sake of both.

The Great Impasse (I feel like that season needs a name) was really a struggle between short-term and long-term benefits. I was sad, I was tired, I was angry, and we were broke. My quick fix to our problems was to leave the country. (Honestly, that's my go-to remedy for most ailments. Have a problem? Pull out that passport!) But Carl could see that while this was a good short-term fix, our future selves would not be thrilled with that decision. Carl had his eyes on the future. But we also don't want to completely forsake our enjoyment of the present to prioritize the future. We know the future isn't guaranteed, so we don't want to put off a life we love.

People used to work their whole lives in preparation for retirement. They would work forty years for the same company, then retire, receive a pension, buy a house in Florida, and play a lot of golf. That was the reward at the end of their long journey. A lot of people lived a life they didn't love all that much so that eventually, they could live a life they did.

But many of us have seen that story fall apart.

Carl and I, for example, graduated from college during the height of the Great Recession. As we applied for our first jobs, we found ourselves competing against wildly overqualified people who were at the end of their careers. They were either about to retire or already retired, and they'd lost all their money in the recession—so there they were, starting over, going back to work and competing with twenty-two-year-olds for entry-level positions.

We watched wonderful, wise adults lose all their retirement savings in a heartbeat after working their whole lives, and that's not something you just get over.

We've also seen people we love have their health taken away from them much too early. They have the funds to retire, but not the health to enjoy it.

Living through a global pandemic was the final tipping point for us in a lot of ways. It solidified our belief that we don't want to save all our enjoyment of life for the end—because sometimes, unexpected things happen along the way.

I also just cannot get on board with the idea that the only way to love the future is to hate the present. If the trade-off really works that way, then I'd rather love the future a little less and like the present a little more today. I'd rather even it out than prioritize one and completely sacrifice the other. That's been our philosophy—but as you work together, the two of you will find your own.

Creating a life you love is challenging. Creating a life you both love and doing it together—that's even harder. So if you're feeling stuck or frustrated or discouraged, know that you're not alone. But keep working together. Keep talking. Keep listening. Take turns, trade off, keep your eyes on your shared definition of success, and keep working together to get there.

And know that together, you get to decide. There's no one right way to build a life, whether as an individual or as a couple. Together, you get to build a life you're excited about and proud of, a life that looks and feels like *you*—both of you. And while it's not an easy journey, it's a beautiful one, and the destination is more than worth it.

CHAPTER THIRTEEN

CHANGE OF PLANS

So, here's the good news and the bad news: The process of creating a life you love isn't a onetime thing. It's not like solving a puzzle, where you work hard to put each piece exactly where it's supposed to go and then once you're done, you're done.

Remember that instead, you're putting together a collage. You might put together one side of it, but then something changes, so you make some room, shifting pieces around. Or maybe you build something beautiful, but then right as you're putting on the finishing touches you have a whole new idea—something you didn't think of right away.

Or you might wake up one day and realize that the overall picture you created just doesn't serve you the way it once did. You need, or maybe just want, something different. Or maybe something unexpected happens just as you get things arranged exactly as you want them—maybe a pin falls out and all your hard work goes fluttering to the floor.

Life isn't static. It's not a destination we reach, it's a journey we're on—a journey of thoughtfully reimagining our lives over and over as we grow and change, and as the world changes around us.

One of the hardest parts about creating a life you love, though, is that the events of our lives don't always happen when or how we want them to. Because our desires and hopes usually involve other people, it can feel like we don't have authority over our lives after all.

Maybe you know exactly what you want to do for your career. Either you've known it for years, or else you've tried a variety of options and feel like you've finally found what you're meant to do. You've honed your skills and done as much networking as your introvert-self can muster, you've applied and interviewed and put yourself out there, and it just is not happening.

You're starting to wonder if maybe you picked the wrong path, or more painfully, if you're not good enough for the path you picked.

You thought you got to choose—that you get to decide what you want to do with your life. But now it feels like someone else gets to decide for you. You can't force them to hire you; you can't make them make your dreams come true.

It's the same with dating and relationships. You can't just snap your fingers and have the perfect person show up on your doorstep. (If you could, you would have done that a long time ago, right?) It feels like you're at the mercy of an infuriating cocktail of God, timing, luck, and your future person (wherever they are), and you just have to wait until they all miraculously come together.

Maybe you've had a few serious relationships with people you thought could be "the one"—they were almost it, so close, but just not quite. No matter how much you squinted and tried and hoped you could make it work, you finally had to admit to yourself, and then to them, that you knew this wasn't it.

Or maybe you've put yourself out there—you've gone on a ton of first dates that never seem to turn into more. You know the right person must be out there somewhere, but the more "wrong" people you meet, the harder it is to hold on to hope.

Or maybe, more than anything, you want to be a mom. Having kids is one of your most central dreams for your life. You have baby names picked out, and wallpaper for the nursery, and there might just be a small collection of baby clothes in a box under your bed.

You have other desires and wants for your life, certainly. But those are more like silhouettes—they're fuzzy and out of focus. The thing you know you want to be true about your life—the one detail of your future that you have imagined a thousand times—is what it will be like to be a mom, to have kids of your own. For you, your Everything Era isn't heavy with indecision; it's heavy with expectation, with the weight of hopes and dreams you can't wait to see realized.

But I found out the hard way that just because you decide you're ready to have a baby, doesn't mean you get to have a baby. It felt like a cruel joke.

For a long time, Carl and I weren't sure we wanted to have kids, and then, for even longer, we just weren't ready. So we waited until we were totally sure and completely ready—but then, when we did start trying, it simply didn't happen.

Realistically, I knew that it takes couples an average of six months to get pregnant. But my high school health class had left me with the impression that getting pregnant was *easy*. (Like, if you kiss a boy in a hot tub, for example, you should probably take a pregnancy test. Just in case.) So I'd arrived in adulthood with the expectation that my reproductive system was raring to go, just barely being held back by birth control—and the second we pulled the goalie, that would be it.

But of course, that's not how it happened.

We first started trying in June. As my cycle came to a close, I watched the days pass like a hawk. Every second seemed to stretch on for hours, and every hour seemed to stretch on for days. I consulted my newly downloaded pregnancy apps multiple times a day, reading and rereading about the earliest symptoms.

I was pretty sure I had that symptom, and this one too. And was I oddly hungry? And "Do you smell that too? Or is that me being super sensitive to smells now that I may or may not be, but probably am, pregnant?"

I daydreamed about what it would be like to take that positive pregnancy test, how we'd surprise our parents with the news. I had it all figured out. I could picture it perfectly. I was sure this was the moment—and then just like that, it wasn't.

I found out that first month that early pregnancy symptoms and PMS symptoms can be exactly the same. They're indistinguishable for most women—and so I was left playing the meanest guessing game ever for weeks each month.

I wasn't pregnant that first month, and I wasn't pregnant the second. I wasn't pregnant the sixth or the ninth or the twelfth.

This type of disappointment can happen in many different areas of our lives. We spend time and effort figuring out what we want and making just the right plan, but when we finally convince ourselves to take that first brave step forward . . . crickets. Nothing. The thing we so badly want does not happen. It turns out that it's totally outside our control, or at least it feels that way.

This might seem like a dagger to the heart of everything we've been talking about so far. How are you supposed to create a life you love when you're doing all you can and it's not working? How are you supposed to create a life you love, to make decisions creatively, to exercise your authority over your life when it turns out you can't actually control all the factors?

You can't make that person love you, you can't make that

company hire you, you can't make yourself get pregnant, you can't make that house be available, you can't make that person be friends with you. It might feel like you're back in a holding pattern, praying for the life of your dreams to find you and feeling helpless to do anything else.

I know how consuming and disheartening that helplessness can feel—but recently, I've been learning some helpful tools for moving forward in these situations. These lessons have come from an unexpected source: my daughter Annie.

Annie is three, and she has strong opinions about everything: "I want the green cup, not the pink cup!" "I want the banana *in* the peel." "I sit on *this* side of the car." "I want to put on my shoes. No, *those* shoes." She's kind and warm and smart and hilarious, but toddlers are *wild*. If you ask a toddler to hand you whatever item they just picked up, but they want to keep it, you know a meltdown is rapidly approaching.

This is especially tricky because the things they're interested in holding always seem to be things a toddler should never have access to. They're often sharp, or electronic in nature, and toddlers always want to put whatever it is into their mouths.

The other day, it was a pencil and Annie was running with it. I asked her to stop, I told her to stop, I more firmly told her to stop. "NO," she told me, so decisively and confidently I couldn't help but be proud. And then I was back to being frustrated. As a parent, it is so irritating how often your kids will not do what you've asked them to do.

But I've been learning that boundaries aren't about what the other person does or doesn't do. Boundaries don't require the other person's compliance at all. Boundaries are about what *you* do.

Here's an example.

"Annie, please stop running with the pencil; it's not safe.

Hey, Annie, please stop running with the pencil! Annie, I asked you to stop running with the pencil, did you hear me? *Annie!*"

This is the moment when many of us would get into a total power struggle. We're telling them to do something, they're saying "no," and we feel helpless because we cannot (seriously, *cannot*) get this strong-willed little person to comply. Sounds like so many parts of the rest of my life, and I'm sure yours too, right?

But when you set a boundary, you decide what you're going to do regardless of what they do. You tell them, and then you do it. "Annie, I cannot let you run with a pencil. It's not safe. If you can't listen, I'm going to take it away." I gave her one more chance, and then I went over and took the pencil away.

Annie can respond however she wants. She can move on and play with something else, or she can have a full-on meltdown. That's up to her, and I'll be there to help her through either. But I've done what I can do. I set the boundary and I stuck to it.

I can't control what my kids do. I can't control what anyone else does. I can only control what I do in response. I get to decide that if my child is doing something dangerous, I am going to step in.

The same principle applies to the other stubborn parts of our lives. We can't control every circumstance. We can't tell another person what to do. But we *can* decide what *we're* going to do—and we have a variety of options to choose from when an area of our life is just not going according to plan.

Quit

One of your options is to quit. You can throw in the towel, stop trying altogether. You can decide that maybe you're just not meant to be married, maybe there isn't a person out there for you. You can decide that while you'd love to have a career in music, it's just not happening, so you're going to make the choice to walk away. You can stop trying to get pregnant.

I'm rarely a fan of quitting. In fact, I'm much more likely to hold on too long than to quit too soon. But that's because I've decided I'd prefer to live with the pain of having tried too long and too hard only to find that I wasn't able to get what I wanted, rather than always wondering what could have happened if I'd just tried a little harder. I'd rather be flat-out rejected than live in the shadow of the what-ifs.

But sometimes, quitting is the kindest, healthiest thing you can do for yourself. Or maybe you don't have to quit permanently, but you do need a break. This has been the case for many of my friends as they've tried to get pregnant. Their lives started to orbit around their ovulation schedules, they couldn't see straight or think about anything else, and they just needed some time away. This is how I felt when I was panicking about getting married. Carl and I decided to pause all marriage talk, and we did that for more than six months. With that pressure off the table, we were able to just be together, to continue getting to know each other. It was incredibly helpful.

Quitting is an option when it comes to your career as well. You don't have to work where you do now. You don't have to stay. You can quit. You can find something else. If you're looking to grow in your career and your current company isn't interested in helping you do that, you can move on and find another company that is.

Just knowing that quitting is an option can be empowering. Only when you realize that you can stop do you have the power to choose to keep going.

Keep Doing What You're Doing

Another option is to keep trying—to keep doing exactly what you're doing and just do it longer. Sometimes, the reason something hasn't happened yet isn't because you're not good enough, or because you're doing it wrong. It's because it just hasn't happened yet.

An average, healthy, thirty-year-old couple has a 20 percent chance of getting pregnant each month they try. Each month, the odds of conception are one in five. So if a couple doesn't get pregnant in a given month, it's not necessarily because they did something wrong or because there's something wrong with them. What they're trying to do doesn't work 100 percent of the time. They just need to try again.

When I was in journalism school, the meteorologist from our local television station came to one of our classes as a guest speaker. She told us her career story, including how she sent out 199 applications before she finally got her first position.

It took her two hundred applications before someone finally said yes. But this didn't mean she wasn't talented. It didn't mean she'd done something wrong or that something was wrong with her. Every station had different needs and different circumstances, and for some of them, she just wasn't the exact right fit. Maybe one station had just hired another person fresh out of school, and they needed someone with more experience to round out their team. At another station, maybe most of their broadcast team was young women with brown hair, and they needed someone different. Maybe her resume got lost, or the position was filled before they got to her resume in the stack. Maybe they were on a hiring freeze. Maybe the job went to a former intern everyone loved. And sure, maybe a few people thought she wasn't good enough, or good enough *yet*. But that didn't mean their opinion was right, or that every station she applied to would feel that way.

She knew the rejections weren't personal, so she kept trying. She kept knocking until a door finally opened—and once she got in, other doors opened more and more easily for the rest of her career. The first door might have been a doozy, but all it took was one.

I love this story and I think of it often. When we're rejected, or even when we're not immediately accepted, we often think that we must have done something wrong, or that there must be something wrong with us. We assume that if we were the right girl for the job, if we were good enough, if this was going to happen for us, that the door would have swung open for us right away.

But most good things take time. Even if a situation ends up being exactly the right fit, it *still* might take time.

Sometimes we just have to keep trying. And again, that's something you can *decide* to do. When faced with stubborn situations, you may not be able to control the outcome, but you can control how long you try. You can decide to keep going on dates until you meet someone great, you can decide to keep trying to get pregnant until it finally works, and you can decide to keep applying for jobs because you know you just need *one* person to give you a shot. You can decide that you're going to be the person who sticks it out with strength, grit, and determination—who keeps knocking on doors until one finally opens. You can keep trying.

Change Tactics

Another thing you can decide to do is change tactics. If you've been trying one way for a while, it might be time to examine your efforts and see if there's anything you can do to make them more effective. Maybe you could rework your resume or try calling instead of emailing, or maybe you could switch to a different dating app or try going out with people who are *not* your usual type.

Carl and I changed tactics several times as we were trying to get pregnant. We tried different nutritional supplements and dietary changes, I did acupuncture for a while, and we used different tests and trackers to make sure we had our timing right. And I can't tell you how many changes I've made along the way in my career.

There's a quote that most people attribute to Einstein: "Insanity is doing the same thing over and over again and expecting different results." Okay, that's not the actual definition of insanity, and it's also likely that Einstein never said that.

But at some point, it does become silly to keep doing the same thing over and over again and expect different results. If you're not getting the result you want, it might be time to change tactics.

There are going to be aspects of your life that you can't control, but you *can* control what you're putting into the equation. Re-evaluating and making some changes to what you're putting in might lead to a different result on the other side.

Don't Skip the Present—Invest in It

Another option when you're feeling stuck is to choose to invest deeply in whatever your life holds in the present—regardless of what might happen in the future. When Carl and I were trying to get pregnant, we felt like our life was on hold. The trying and the waiting and the doctors appointments and the timing of everything felt all-consuming. And it felt like our future was being held hostage as well. We couldn't make any other big decisions, because we'd already made this one and we were still waiting for it to happen. Every future-related conversation came with an aster-isk: "*Plans may get canceled because of pregnancy and/or baby." Future plans felt so tentative, we finally stopped making them.

We all do that—put plans on hold because we're waiting for something else to happen first.

I know I'll meet my person in the next few years, so I'll just put off taking that trip/buying a house/getting a dog until then.

I know we'll be getting pregnant in the next few years, so I'll wait to go back to school/ask for that promotion/pursue that dream until we do.

The problem is, the things we're waiting for don't always happen when we want them to, so we miss out on wonderful experiences because we're constantly putting them off.

The road of life is long. It could be a while before we arrive at our next destination, and most likely, as soon as we get there we'll be setting our sights on a new one. Most of our time is spent on the road rather than feeling like we've arrived. So if we're going to love our lives, we need to learn how to love where we are—to appreciate, savor, and make the most of our lives right in the middle of the journey. Part of creating a life you love is learning to love (and truly live!) your life when you haven't quite gotten where you want to go yet.

When Carl and I bought our first house in Nashville, one of the first questions anyone asked us was whether it was in a good school district. Honestly, we hadn't even thought to check. Once we did check, we discovered our assigned local school wouldn't have been our first choice. But we bought the house anyway, because we had a hunch that we weren't going to live there long enough for it to matter. And we were right. We bought that house eight years ago, and we are *still* three years away from our kids going to kindergarten. We made a decision that was right for the season of life we were in at the time, not for a season that may or may not have come at some point down the road.

This might be one of the hardest parts about creating a life we love—this dance between being in the present and focusing on the future. As we've talked about, sometimes we need to sacrifice a bit of the present for the sake of the future. For example, right now it's five o'clock on a Sunday morning and I'm awake working on this book. I never wake up this early, but in this case, waking up early today is an investment in the future.

Sometimes we might choose to spend less today so we can save for tomorrow. We work hard today so we can rest tomorrow. We take a hit in the short term for the sake of a win in the long term.

But other times, if we focus only on the long term, we miss out on the short term. That would have been the case with our first house. We didn't need a bigger house in a great neighborhood with good schools. A little house in an up-and-coming area of the city was perfect for the phase of life we were in. It was also a great investment. Because we bought that first house, we were able to buy bigger versions later. An investment in the present ended up serving our future well too.

One of the most important things we can do during a stubborn season is to invest in our present moment. I first learned this lesson when I was single and dating. One of the biggest, clearest desires I had for my life was to find somebody to share it with. I didn't always know exactly what I wanted to do for work, I definitely didn't always know I wanted to be a mom, and I didn't always have a clear vision of where I wanted to live, or how I wanted to live, or even who I wanted to be. But the one thing I always knew was that I wanted a great love story. I wanted to find someone amazing and spend the rest of my life with him.

I wanted this for my future with such ferocity, it often took me out of the present. I walked through life in a sort of daze, constantly scheming and dreaming about how I could get to that part of my future faster. In the process, I was missing my life.

But along the way—through making a lot of mistakes, learning the hard way, and receiving guidance from some smart and wonderful people—I finally realized I needed to make a change. I needed to start being present in the present. Some wise mentors showed me that if I could do this, it would be the best thing I could do for my life today and for my life down the road.

It wasn't instantaneous, and it wasn't always easy, but I did start to enjoy my time being single. I invested in myself, my friendships, my dreams, and my faith. I worked to become the woman I'd always wanted to be and to live a life I was proud of—a life I was excited to invite another person into, but that wasn't incomplete because they weren't in it yet.

The things I did while I was single were the reason I was in the right place at the right time to meet Carl—and the reason I was ready for a relationship when it was time. The growing we both did while we were single has made an enormous difference in our marriage. Years later, we're still seeing the impact.

My mom and dad have been married for more than forty years, and even though they've been married for most of their lives, at least once a month my dad tells a story that my mom has never heard before. We'll be at dinner and he'll pull out a story from one of the first jobs he ever had, or a prank he pulled on his brother, or something that happened when he was in the military. And my mom will shake her head and laugh as she says, "I swear, just when I think I know all his stories, there's another one I haven't heard before!"

They've been married for more than forty years and are

still getting to know each other, and it's because they're both interesting people with deep wells of experiences, thoughts, and stories for the other to explore and get to know.

I love hearing about who my parents were before my sister and I came along, and I can't wait to share my stories with my girls too. The time we spend on the road during each leg of our journey is the time we can use to become the people we want to be at our destination. If we're only focused on the future, we run the risk of missing out on all the learning, growth, and experiences we could have in the meantime.

Another thing I've realized is that we don't have guarantees. We don't know that we'll end up getting married, or having kids, or arriving at whatever destination we have circled on the map. I would have been disappointed to miss out on those dreams and goals, but I would have been even more disappointed if I'd missed out on every other part of my life too.

In the midst of trying to get pregnant, Carl and I had the chance to spend two weeks in Italy. We needed some time away, a change of scenery, a chance to connect (ideally over lots and lots of pasta).

So that's what we did. For two weeks we rented a car and drove around Tuscany to all the little towns I'd spent years dreaming about but had never had a chance to see.

But then, a few days into our trip, I realized my period was late. It had never been late before—it was infuriatingly, heartbreakingly punctual. But this time, it wasn't. One day passed, and then another day, and then another. I tried not to get excited. I'd been disappointed for so many months in a row, I didn't want to get my hopes up. But I almost couldn't help it.

This would be the perfect ending to this story. We'd tried and tried, and cried and cried, and then finally, miraculously, while we were in Italy, we'd get our first positive pregnancy test. I pictured going to an Italian *farmacia* to get the test. Maybe the test would say "*si*" or "*incinta*" instead of "yes" or "pregnant." Or maybe it would just—finally—show us two little pink lines where there had always only been one.

But then, as soon as my mind got to the part I'd spent the most time imagining—the part where we'd get to surprise our family with the news—my period started.

A tidal wave of emotions crashed down on me in our little Italian bathroom. I was furious and devastated. I was mad at myself for getting my hopes up *again*. I should have known better by now.

I told Carl the news and then headed for the door—I needed some air.

But the second I stepped outside, I was hit with another thought.

It was a familiar thought, one that had gotten me through a long season of singleness. And it hadn't just gotten me through; it had changed everything for me.

The thought was this: "If you knew that you were going to get everything you've been dreaming of in just a few years, how would you live your life today?"

If I decided to loosen my grip and trust God's plans and timing for my life—truly trust them—then how would I live my life today?

I would make the most of it. I knew the answer before I'd even finished the question.

Now, of course, we don't necessarily get any assurances that what we're dreaming of will happen someday. We don't get a postcard in the mail that says, "Dear Stephanie, I promise I'm working on it. Your dreams will come true and I won't make you wait too long. In the meantime, embrace this season. Use it well. You can trust me, God." (Although, God, if you're open to suggestions, a postcard like that would be *awesome*!)

But I've discovered that when I think about how I'd live if I did have that assurance, and make decisions from that place, I make some of the best decisions of my life.

And so that's what I did.

Refueled by this reminder, I decided that I was going to let that thought change my life all over again. I knew I wouldn't regret embracing this married-without-children season. I knew I'd regret missing out on it.

So Carl and I embraced the season we were in. We fully savored every bite (I mean, every moment) of the time we had left in Italy, and we took some big steps as soon as we got home.

We booked more trips—adventures for the two of us and trips to see and spend time with our people. We kept working hard, building the businesses that would support the life we wanted to invite our kids into whenever the time came. We did house projects and spent time together and with friends—investing in our home and our relationships in a way we might not have time for whenever our next chapter began. I went back to therapy and dug through some unhealthy behavior patterns (like people-pleasing and lack of boundaries) that had plagued me my whole life and that I just didn't want to carry around anymore.

We couldn't control the timing of when—or if—we were going to get pregnant, but there were plenty of things we could do in the meantime, and I knew we would never regret doing them. If we were never able to have kids, these were things we would have wanted to spend our time doing anyway. I would have hated to look back and realize we'd missed out not just on having kids but on how we could have spent the years of waiting. And if we did end up being able to have kids, we were helping build the world we wanted to bring them into—and I was becoming the kind of person I wanted to be when they arrived.

But, just because we decided to make the most of the present didn't mean we gave up on the future. We definitely didn't do that. Instead, we realized that we'd done all we knew how to do on our own, and it was time to ask for some help.

Ask for Help

After we got home from Italy, I still had my newfound resolve to make the most of our current season. But I also called and made an appointment with a fertility specialist.

When we're doing everything we can and it's still not working, that's a great indication that it's time to ask for some help. So many of us think we should be able to figure life out on our own. But that's just not the truth.

Over the last ten years or so, I've learned that strength isn't proving that I can do it on my own. It's knowing that I don't have to and then surrounding myself with the best people, resources, and tools possible—especially in areas of my life that I care about deeply.

If an area of your life isn't going the way you want it to, this might be the perfect time to ask for some help. That might look like reading a book, taking a class, or attending a workshop. It might look like enlisting the help of a coach, mentor, or therapist.

It's hard to ask for help, and it can sometimes even be expensive. But what's this area of your life worth to you? How badly do you want it to be different? That's a question only you can answer.

I'm forever grateful that we asked for help on our fertility journey. Yes, we could have continued to try to get pregnant on our own, and maybe it would have worked eventually. That would have been the less costly route, I suppose—financially, at least.

But we were discovering that the process of trying and hoping and waiting and being progressively more disappointed every month was costing us in many other ways. It was taking a toll on our hearts, minds, and bodies, and on our relationship.

And while it had taken a while for us to decide that we wanted to be parents, now that we were sure, we were truly sure. We'd thought about it every which way. We'd examined the possibilities, the options, the potential paths our life could take, and we'd intentionally chosen this one. We weren't on the fence anymore. So finally, we asked for help.

I'll never forget that first meeting with our fertility doctor. We walked in armed with information: *This is when I think my last cycle started and stopped and how long I think it was. I took my temperature this morning and yesterday and this is what it said.* I'd been tracking every detail about my body for more than a year at that point, and I was ready to catch my doctor up on all that I knew.

But he held up a hand and said gently, "Stephanie, we're past all that. I can take it from here."

My eyes immediately filled with tears. I was so relieved. I'd been playing the role of totally unqualified expert for more than a year, and I was exhausted. The idea that I could just relax and let someone else lead the way for a while was the most welcome relief. That's what I've often found about asking for help.

When you find someone who can lead the way in an important area of your life, you get to breathe and just be a participant for a while. You get to follow instructions and feel your feelings and rest in the assurance that someone else has a plan—someone who knows a heck of a lot more about the topic at hand than you do.

So asking for help is another great next step you can decide to take, and it's a choice only you can make. Do you still have more tricks up your sleeve, ideas you want to try before you call in reinforcements? Or are you exhausted, like I was, ready for someone else to take the lead for a while?

One of the most helpful sources of outside help I've found along the way is therapy. Often, the things holding us back from creating a life we love are internal rather than external. We've tried everything we can to get past that mental block, to wriggle out of those suffocating thought patterns, to forgive and move on after being hurt, and we just haven't been able to. A therapist can help us process our mental and emotional clutter, heal from trauma and past experiences, identify strategies for overcoming unhelpful patterns, and see potential paths forward that we never would have thought of on our own. That's why I'm grateful for therapy.

I'm so glad I don't have to create a life I love on my own, and I'm so glad you don't have to either. You really don't. You can ask for help, and I hope you do.

Getting What You Hoped For

Like I said, Carl and I tried for years to get pregnant, and it just wasn't happening. We finally enlisted the help of our wonderful doctors, underwent a battery of tests, and tried several different kinds of treatments and medications. Still, none of it worked. We were officially diagnosed with "unexplained infertility."

Eventually, we decided to try IVF, and after a ton of time and money, a zillion doctor's appointments, and even more injections, we found ourselves with one healthy embryo. Just one. We were so grateful to have one, but also nervous because having only one meant no second chance. It also meant no potential for a second baby, or so we thought.

A few weeks after our embryo transfer, we were elated when we finally got our two pink lines. "You're pregnant!" our nurse confirmed, and she scheduled our first ultrasound.

Two weeks later, our doctor talked us through the ultrasound. "Do you see this?" he asked us. "This is the baby, and this is their heartbeat." He was just about to finish up when something else caught his eye. He stopped, looked, moved the ultrasound wand around a little, and looked again. "Okay, kids." He paused. "You see this, right? This is a baby; this is its heartbeat." He moved the ultrasound wand again. "Now, you see this, right? This is a baby; this is its heartbeat."

"*Wait, what?*" We were still catching up.

"This is a baby, and this is a baby. Guys . . . you're having twins." Our one precious embryo had split into two—a total miracle and a better ending to our story than we ever could have written on our own.

Thirty-one weeks later, we welcomed identical twin girls into the world: Annie and Quinn Wilson.

Some days, I still can't believe this is how our story turned out. The girls are three now. They're wild and hilarious and endlessly fun. They're smart and warm and deeply kind. I like them so much and I love them so much, and it's the great honor of my life to lead this little tribe of women. I'm so glad I get to be their mom.

I tell you this story because sometimes, often, our plans don't go according to plan. This is both maddening and heartbreaking, and if you're there right now, I want you to know you're not alone. I also hope it helps you as much as it's helped me to be reminded that while you can't control your situation completely, you *do* have options. You can quit, walk away, leave it behind, and move forward with a fresh start. You can keep going—dig in your heels and decide that you're in it for the long haul and are going to keep trying until something changes. You can change tactics— examine your efforts, see what's been working and what hasn't, and make changes accordingly. Whatever you decide, I hope you make the most of the meantime, since that's where we spend so much of our lives. And, last but certainly not least, you can ask for help.

You can't control everything, but these things you can control, and often they make all the difference in the world. I know they did for us.

CHAPTER FOURTEEN

DECISIONS YOU HAVE TO REMAKE OR REIMAGINE

Unfortunately and fortunately, the process of creating a life you love isn't a onetime thing. You can get everything arranged perfectly, but inevitably something changes. Life changes, circumstances change, *you* change. And the life that once fit you like a glove now fits like a pair of old nonstretch jeans straight out of the dryer—you can get into them, technically, but only after a lot of wiggling and lying on the floor, and potentially some help from a friend.

Or maybe the life you built is much too big, too bulky, too heavy—like getting all dressed up in ski gear and then trying to go on a date. You're sweating under layers of long underwear and puffy pants, not to mention the gloves, scarf, hat, and goggles. You're so hot and weighed down, so busy managing all the layers, you don't have the time or energy to be present for the life unfolding around you.

And it seems crazy, because the life you built did fit at one point. The choices you made were the exact thing you needed at the time you made them. When you chose that apartment, took that job, got into that relationship, committed to that decision—it was right. But now, it's just not.

The Great Undoing

As I write this, I'm sitting on the floor of a rental house in a sub-
urb thirty minutes north of Nashville. We live here now, and if
you would have told me six months ago that this is how our story
would unfold, I would not have believed you.

We'd just moved into our dream house. I never in a thousand
years thought I'd give it up so quickly—and I never could have
imagined how proud I'd be of us for making that decision.

But let me back up. We've lived in Nashville for almost ten
years now, and for most of that time, we lived in a lovely little
house in a neighborhood we just adored.

It was a medium-sized house, not tiny but not huge, and
while we weren't ready to have kids at the time we bought it, we
knew exactly which room would be the nursery when the time
came. It would be the perfect home for a family of three. We
thought we might want to get something a little bigger before
we had our second baby, but we figured that was a long way off.

It was a long, thin house—it looked like a townhome that
was just slightly disconnected from its neighbors—and it had
a great double front porch, with a front porch downstairs and a
balcony right on top of it. The house faced downtown Nashville,
and on the fourth of July we could see fireworks in the distance,
crackling and popping over the heart of the city.

It was in a great neighborhood, one of the best in Nashville,
I think. It's the kind of neighborhood that people are just starting to realize is great. It has great restaurants, breweries, and
shops—all walking distance from our house—but because it's
an old industrial area that people only recently began moving into, it flies under the radar compared to other popular
Nashville spots.

We were in that house for four years, and I thought we'd be there much longer—until we found out that we were pregnant with not one baby, but two.

Everything changed when the twins were born. Of course it did. I knew it would, but I was still somehow caught totally unprepared. We'd built such a beautiful life—piece by piece, decision by decision. I was so excited to invite the girls into it. I figured we'd make some space for them in our little house. We decorated our nursery with care and set it up with all the little things we thought two babies could possibly need. We made room in our schedules too. We prepared to take a month or so off from work over Christmas, figuring we'd be able to slowly start working from home again in the new year.

For as much as I'd worried about becoming the default stay-at-home parent, we hadn't put that much effort into lining up childcare. Granted, the girls were born during the height of the pandemic, so Carl and I were both nervous to bring other people around our brand-new babies. We were also both working from home with tons of job flexibility. We figured we'd trade off and work while they napped, and we also knew we'd have a day or two of help each week from Carl's parents (bless them!). *We'll be able to do it all*, we thought. *No reason to worry.*

Boy, were we wrong. Maybe it's the fact that there were two of them, or the fact that their health was extra fragile because they were born slightly early. Maybe it's the fact that we were new parents and had no clue what we were doing, or the fact that we were still in the peak of the pandemic, but our lives and home and schedule were turned so far upside down, they were almost unrecognizable.

First of all, we had seriously underestimated how much stuff the girls were going to need. Overnight, every corner of our house became a baby zone—diaper-changing stations, bottle-filling stations, nursing stations, pumping stations. So much for our beautiful nursery. The whole house became the nursery. We were lucky if there was still room for us in it.

Our schedules were also thrown totally out of whack. Because the girls were underweight, we had to feed them every three hours around the clock for months. And because there were two of them, and because we didn't know what we were doing, and because they were having a hard time eating, feeding them took a full ninety minutes. For months, neither Carl nor I got more than ninety minutes of sleep at a time. For months.

We were in such survival mode at the beginning, we all but forgot about our jobs. (Thank goodness for our teams who kept things together!) For at least six weeks, neither of us had a clue where our laptops even were, let alone what emails we might need to respond to or work we might need to do. It wasn't because we had carved out a leisurely season of family leave, either. (Is there such a thing?) We were so far underwater, we couldn't have worked even if our jobs depended on it.

Basically, we discovered that the life we had created wasn't going to work anymore, and so we were quickly faced with two big decisions:

One: Where were we going to live? Two babies, two adults, and two full-time jobs were not going to fit in our little house. And two: Speaking of full-time jobs, now that we knew taking care of the girls was a full-time job in and of itself, who was going to work, who was going to take care of them, and how were we going to make both the schedule and the finances fit?

The answer to the first question felt easier. We always figured we'd buy a bigger house at some point (and it was a viable option with where the housing market was at the time). Our life had expanded so much, so quickly, we figured this was our moment. We could use more space, it would be nice to have a place we could grow into and stay in for a while, and if we found a place in a good school district, we could theoretically stay in our new house for years and years without having to move again. We thought a bigger house was the best way to take care of our little family.

We were excited about the prospect, and proud of ourselves for being in a position to be able to make it happen. We'd come a long way! So, we began searching for a bigger house.

The second thing we had to figure out was who was going to work and who was going to take care of the girls. For a while we really thought we could do both—that if we just optimized our schedules enough, worked smart enough, and traded off throughout the day, we'd both be able to work full-time and also take care of our babies with only a little outside help. (At least for a while!)

The first day I tried to go back to work—and by that, I mean do just a tiny bit of work for the first time in months—I was so excited to get back to it. We put the babies down for a nap, Carl went downstairs to take a call with a client, and I went to the bathroom, refilled my coffee, sat down at my computer, and wrote one single paragraph before . . . both babies woke up. I snuck into their room, hoping I'd be able to quickly coax them back to sleep. I wanted to finish my email (and my cup of coffee before it got cold!). But I quickly discovered that not only were they awake, they both wanted to be picked up and they wanted to be picked up *now*. There was no way they were going to fall back to sleep. I knew Carl was on an important call and that I needed to at least try to keep the girls somewhat quiet. But picking up and soothing two tiny babies at the same time is remarkably difficult when you only have two arms. So, trying a new tactic, I put the girls on the floor and crouched down over them, wrapping my arms around both of them, shushing them as they wailed, and wailing myself as I counted the minutes until Carl got off of his phone call. Forty-five minutes later, he sprinted up the stairs and found me and the babies lying on the floor together—all three of us still crying.

Yeah . . . this wasn't going to work.

I'd spent my whole life believing (or maybe just *really* hoping) that it was possible to do it all—to have a great career and be a great mom—and I still believe it is. But now I know that it's not possible without help. Taking care of two babies is more than a full-time job (especially in the early months!), and so we had a choice: either one of us needed to quit our job and focus on the girls full-time, or else we needed to hire someone to help.

But that choice was complicated too, because hiring someone to help us was much easier said than done. It turns out, finding a great babysitter isn't like ordering a pizza. You don't just call for help and have it in thirty minutes or less. We started searching, and interviewing, and asking friends of friends. It felt like online dating. I lost count of the number of awkward phone interviews, and how many times we thought we'd found someone we liked but then never heard from them again.

Daycare wasn't any easier. I called around to try to find space for the girls, only to discover that I should have gotten us on a waiting list the second I found out I was pregnant—and even that might have been too late. It was going to be at least two years before we could get spots.

And then there was the question of paying for it. When you're thinking about having kids, you know it's going to be expensive, and you know that one of the most challenging expenses will be paying for college eventually. But what I didn't know to expect was the fact that childcare (even part-time!) was going to cost roughly the same as a year of in-state college tuition—without the eighteen years to save for it ahead of time.

Finally, we found both an amazing new house and a wonderful nanny, and for the first time, I felt like maybe we were going to be okay. We could both keep working, the girls were being taken care of by someone amazing, and we had enough space in our new house for us all to be there together—Carl doing his work, me doing mine, and our wonderful new nanny taking care of the girls. We loved being able to keep tabs on how the girls were doing throughout the day, lend a hand if they needed something, and go see them for a few minutes every time we had a break between meetings.

It really was a total dream—dream house, dream childcare situation that afforded us the time and space to do our dream jobs—until we realized just how much this dream life was going to cost us, and the fact that we might not actually be able to afford both the help and the house we thought we needed.

We Changed All the Variables and It Still Wasn't Working

The dream life we'd built for ourselves was too big and far too expensive. Carl and I each felt like we were trying to take care of two babies and two businesses and a big house while wearing a too-bulky, too-hot ski suit. We were sweating and stressed and overwhelmed—our frantic efforts to maintain our new life ended up robbing us of the very peace, rest, and family connection we'd been looking for when we made all these changes in the first place. We were living the dream we'd worked so hard to build, but feeling totally crushed by the cost of it.

One night Carl and I were standing in the kitchen, looking at our budget and wondering how in the world we were going to make it all work. With a new house, childcare bills that cost the same as a new house, and other variables we hadn't even known to expect, our expenses had skyrocketed, and our income wasn't able to keep pace. Now instead of living comfortably within our means, we were scrambling to make enough to support our life—and we were coming up short.

We talked again about what it would be like for one of us to stay home with the girls. If we were able to cut childcare out of the equation, would that make the math work? The answer was no. We would lose more in that equation than we'd save. The numbers still didn't add up.

The fixed elements in our picture were our jobs and our home. (And our family, of course! They were a given). We'd already made significant changes to the variables in our lifestyle—we'd cut out all the extras and thrown overboard everything that wasn't nailed down. Our fixed elements were all that was left.

Finally, Carl spoke the words that felt like our only option. "One or both of us needs to get a different job, Steph." He was right. If we were going to keep our life as it was, we had to make more money to support it. We had to make a change.

And Carl was suggesting that we change one of our fixed elements: our work.

Now, for some people, this would totally make sense.

Say, for example, that you don't love your job. It's okay, but it's not your dream job by any means. If that were the case, the idea of having to make a change in your career might feel scary but also somehow freeing—an idea you hadn't considered, but now you can't believe you didn't think of it sooner.

That was not the case for us.

If we changed jobs, Carl would have to give up his stake as an owner and partner in the company he'd been working for years to build. He'd have to stop working with people he enjoyed and respected—and severely disrupt their lives in the process.

If he walked away from his work now, it would be like building half a house and then abandoning it. You'd never get to see it completed, you'd never get to see it become the thing you always knew it could be, and you'd never get to enjoy the fruits of your labor.

My little business, on the other hand, is the character in this story that I've loved the longest. My business predates Carl, my girls, and any place we've called home. For me, my business isn't just a paycheck; it was my first baby. It's the reason I jump out of bed in the morning—I can't wait to dive in. It's the thing I wake up in the middle of the night thinking about—not because I'm stressed, but because I love thinking about it and I have a thousand and one ideas. My business isn't just a job; it's the work I feel I'm meant to do in the world. So my work was not something I was willing to just walk away from.

As I stared back at Carl, considering his words—"We need to get different jobs, Steph"—I knew that our home wasn't the fixed element I wanted to protect. Our work was.

So we turned to our other fixed element: our home. Should we move? Could we move? The idea was such a radical left turn, we couldn't believe we were considering it.

We loved this house. It was our dream house! It felt like we had finally just gotten settled. We bought this house so we could stay in it for a long time. We couldn't possibly leave it . . . or could we?

As we talked about it, we realized our home wasn't quite as fixed as we thought it was.

For some people, their home may truly be nonnegotiable. Maybe you live on the absolute perfect block in the perfect city in a home that you want to be your home until your kids grow up and go to college. Or maybe you live in your childhood home, a house your grandpa built, or next door to your parents.

None of those things are true for us. Our home is new to us. It fits us, it's beautiful, we love it, and we could stay there forever. But I don't know that we will. Even if it's our forever home, I don't know that forever needs to start now.

And that brings us to today. We spent so much time and effort building a beautiful life in a beautiful home, and now we're dismantling it all.

We put our dream house up for rent, and in the process realized we could make more money for our house if we rented it furnished. So instead of packing up our lives and bringing all our belongings with us, we left most of our things behind. We packed up our beds and the girls' toys, along with the mementos we love the most and the random furniture pieces we love the least (we left all the pretty stuff for our renters!), and we rented a house for ourselves thirty minutes north of Nashville. Our dream house looks exactly as we left it, as we created it for our family, but now a different family lives in it, and we live in a house that, while it's perfectly fine, doesn't look much like us.

Our new house is smaller and, blessedly, less expensive. And best of all, it's close to Carl's parents. We're also just down the street from Annie and Quinn's new preschool, and their grandparents live right in between the school and our house. Carl's parents can pick the girls up from school, or we can stop by their house as we're walking home. I hadn't known to dream up this version of our lives, but I'm so glad we got creative enough to discover a different way of living.

While I feel sad about letting go of the previous version of our lives—whether just for a season or maybe even forever—the possibilities this change opens up for us are so exciting.

For years, I dreamed about bigger and better—collecting, curating, decorating, and finding bigger and bigger spaces to call home. But now I'm dreaming about life with less—less to carry, less to worry about, less to keep up with, less to pay for. Lightening our load has left me with more room in my mind, in my heart, on my to-do list, and in my soul. It's been such a good feeling that we're ready to downsize even further. We're asking questions like, "How much lighter could life feel if we went a little bit smaller, or a lot smaller? How much stuff do we actually need?" We're looking around at the possessions we've accumulated over the years, and while some of them are treasures I wouldn't dream of saying goodbye to, others are just baggage—things I'm tired of carrying around and would be happy to let go of now that I realize that's an option.

By renting out our house, we're able to bring in some additional income, a welcome relief in a season of life that is still *so* expensive. Also, in renting out our house—even if just for a season—we're able to ask and answer the questions "Where do we want to live?" and "What *could* this next season of life look like?" in a whole new way.

What If We Moved to Spain?

"What if we moved to Spain for a year?" I asked in a conversation with Carl one day. I threw the question out almost as a joke. (Too soon?) We were in the thick of playing Tetris with our work, childcare, budget, and schedules, and each scenario seemed more frustratingly not-quite-right than the last. So far, the options we'd been playing with for how to make it all work were variations of different muted blues, and the option I'd just thrown out was a bright lemon yellow.

I love Spain. Have I mentioned that? Some of the best, most pivotal moments of my life have happened in Spain. It's sacred ground for me, the place where my soul both rests and comes alive in a way it doesn't anywhere else. I love the Spanish culture, and I love the Spanish language. I started learning Spanish when I was just ten years old, and it's been a lifelong dream of mine to speak such good Spanish, I can pass for a local. (My Spanish is good, but I have a long way to go!) I've also *always* wanted my kids to speak Spanish, and I've been dreaming about living in Spain with my family for years. But I felt like it was probably a far-fetched dream, at least until our kids were older. Most people don't move to a new country with twin toddlers, and probably for good reason.

But to my total surprise, Carl was actually into the idea. And the more we talked about it, the more research we did, the more we realized that it wasn't such a crazy idea after all. This time, it wasn't a dream that was out of budget and out of reach. It was actually very much within reach—a logistical challenge, sure, but definitely doable—and it was a unique solution to many of the problems we were facing. It was also within budget. At the moment, the cost of living in Spain is less than it is in the US, so it would be a way for us to significantly lower our cost of living, as well as give the girls a chance to learn a second language—a priceless opportunity!

Maybe lemon yellow is our color after all?

I've spent so many years striving for more, thinking that bigger was better in so many ways. For one, I thought our family would be better off in a bigger house. But along the way, I forgot to ask why: What's the point? Why am I doing this? What am I trying to achieve, and is this the only way to do it? Who told me it had to be this way, and is there any other way to live our lives—a way that might fit me and my family even better? I think there is, and at least for the next year, that looks like picking up our family and trying out life somewhere else for a while.

Both of our family's moves, first out of the city and then out of the country, will require us to live with less. We're living in smaller spaces, and we'll have sold or put into storage most of our stuff. But I'm excited for a season of less because it will give us space for so much more—more freedom and flexibility, more breathing room—in our finances, our schedules, and our souls.

It does feel a little bit weird to be dismantling our dream life. And I know that what we build next might look significantly less impressive to someone peeking into our lives from the outside.

Renting a little place well outside the city doesn't look as good on paper as owning a big place right in the heart of it. And taking our toddlers across the ocean to rent an even smaller place in a country where we don't know anybody might look to some like we're making a gigantic mistake. ("Kids need stability. Is that a good idea? Is it safe? And will they even remember your time there? Shouldn't you wait until they're older?")

But I know, and I'm constantly reminding myself, that we're the ones who get to decide, and I'm so proud of us for doing just that. With a generous helping of both authority and creativity, we've chosen this adventure for this next season of our lives, and I cannot *wait*.

Re-Creating a Life You Love

Now, your next steps likely don't include giving up your house and moving across the ocean, and that's okay. Your next steps don't have to be drastic, and they don't have to be the same as mine. A beautiful life isn't one-size-fits-all. The important thing is that you're able to be honest with yourself—able to recognize when something's not working and creative enough to find something else that will.

And the decisions you make today do not have to be the decisions you make tomorrow. If you walk down a certain road and discover (or just decide) that it isn't right for you, you can do something different. You're allowed to change your mind.

Your process doesn't have to be perfect, and your decisions don't have to be perfect. Creating a life you love is an ongoing practice of participating in the creation of your life, making authentic decisions that line up with your values and vision for the future—and you'll continue to do that for the rest of your life.

A beautiful life is something you can build and rebuild as often as you need to. With each new version you create, you'll find that it gets easier to listen to yourself, to identify your needs and respond accordingly. It gets a little bit easier to be creative, to assemble the pieces that for you are just right but for others might be a mismatch. It gets a little bit easier to exercise your authority over your life and to live it authentically—to build and create a life you love, a life that looks and feels like you.

THINGS TO REMEMBER AS YOU CREATE A LIFE YOU LOVE

The Everything Era is hard, isn't it? But it's not hard because you're bad at it. It's hard because it's been that way for women for years and years. If women's progress throughout history was a train, in some ways you're both the caboose and the engine—following a long line of women who have gone (and lived under immense amounts of pressure) before you, and also leading the way down a path few have walked before.

But you're not alone. You're not the only one struggling with the decisions and transitions of this big, important season, and you also don't have to figure it out by yourself. In fact, I hope you don't even try to. Life is much too hard and important and beautiful to go through by ourselves. So gather your people and hold them close. Ask for help early and often. Tell the truth about how you're feeling, what you're going through, and what you need. You're not the only one who needs help, and when you're brave and vulnerable enough to admit how you're doing, you're giving other people permission to do the same. That's the only way we can all be in this together.

The Everything Era isn't easy, but it is certainly beautiful. Today, right now, you have the opportunity to build a life you love. You get to ask and answer questions like, "What do I really want? What will bring me joy? What do I want my life to feel like on the inside—not just look like on the outside? What kind of future do I want to build, and who do I want to build it with?"

There's not one right way to build a life. You get to decide. You don't have to forfeit things that are good and true about you in an attempt to squeeze yourself into a life you don't actually want to live. You get to figure out who you are, what makes you you, and then be you with your whole heart—building a life you're excited about and proud of, a life that's a beautiful reflection of the woman who chose it, a life that looks and feels like you.

And when we do this, not only are we creating a life we love—a life that's creative and authentic and free—we're also paving the way for other women to do the same. We're showing our little sisters, our nieces, our daughters, and our granddaughters who a woman can be and what a woman can do. We're showing them that girls can do anything (but don't have to do everything, thank goodness!). We're opening up a world of possibilities in a kaleidoscope of different colors.

You're brave, and strong, and good, and worthy of a life you love. And I'm cheering you on every step of the way as you pursue exactly that.

All my love,

Stephanie May Wilson

ACKNOWLEDGMENTS

I have to say, writing my acknowledgments feels a bit like writing in my best friend's high school yearbook. It always felt like there was no way I was going to be able to do our friendship justice. Writing my acknowledgments feels just about the same. But here I am. I'm going to do my best.

I am so much better because of the people in my life. I'm kinder, funnier, stronger, more successful, and infinitely wiser because of the women (and men!) who are in my corner, and the same is true of this book. This book would not have happened and would certainly be nowhere near as good without the people who have been in my corner every step of the way.

First, let's talk about my team.

To Carly Kellerman: First my editor, now my agent, and forever my friend. We've walked through our Everything Era together—everything from career, to marriage, to kids, to childcare, to where we want to live, to how we want to live, to who we want to be. We've created lives we love, and we've done it together, and every bit of the journey has been better because I've gotten to do it all with you by my side.

Not only did we walk through our Everything Era together, but you helped me write a book about it. Thirteen years ago we sat in a tent together, whispering late into the night about how I wanted to write books and you wanted to publish books, and we vowed that one day we'd create a book together. We did it. We actually did it! To say this book wouldn't have happened without you is a profound understatement. You were the one who told me I was ready to do this, and who helped me believe it for myself. You held my hand, led the way, carried me, and laughed with me throughout this whole process. I could not have done this without you, and even if I could have, I wouldn't have wanted to. You and I had a hunch all those years ago that we might just be a dream team, and I think we were totally right. Thank you x10000. I cannot wait to see what we cook up next!

To Katie Painter, Carolyn McCready, Amanda Halash, Keren Baltzer, Matt Bray, Morgan Mitchell, and my whole team at Zondervan Books. Thank you so much for your time, your intentionality, your love, your encouragement, and your hard work. What a gift to get to work with such talented, wonderful people.

To Kate Morris, my podcast producer and righthand gal, who kept the rest of our corner of the internet going while I worked on this book. You are a gem. I am so thankful to have you on my team.

To my cabinet: Michelle, Kelsey, Shannon, Amanda, Carly, Kacie, Hanna, Marri, Emily, Heather, and Suzy. What would I do without you guys? You have been my pals and my most trusted advisors throughout this Everything Era. Thank God we got to go through it together. To write and think and grow and learn and mom and live alongside all of you has made me a better person (and a better author!). You are brilliant, brilliant women, and I *love* getting to pursue our dreams together.

(And an extra big thank-you to Kacie and Marri for letting me dump this manuscript in your laps more than once. Your edits and insight were invaluable. You both made this book so much better!)

To my family: To my mom and dad for paving the way, for being such an incredible example of what a life can look like, and for encouraging me endlessly no matter what twists and turns my story has taken. I grew up knowing that I could do anything. What incredible parents you are. To Kelly, Phil, Myla, Zack, Lily, and Rachel—you are the best family in the world. I love you all so much and I'm endlessly inspired by each of you.

To Rob and Kathy: You both have supported me and our family in such real, practical, helpful ways throughout this process. Thank you for all your hours of unpaid babysitting and for the countless meals you've brought us. Thank you for believing in me and cheering me on. Thank you also for inspiring me and setting such a beautiful example for our family to follow. You live such intentional, thoughtful, warm, beautiful lives. Thank you for showing us what's possible.

Now, I've saved the best for last:

Annie and Quinn: I know you're still a little bit too young to understand what mama's been up to, typing away in her office all these months, but you've been an integral part of this. When I found out that I was having girls, I was immediately elated and intimidated. I knew that with the way I live my life in front of you, I'd be giving you the most up-close example you'll ever have of what it means to be a woman. With my life and with this book, I hope I'm showing you that you can do anything. (And anything is not the same as everything! You do *not* have to do everything!) Being a woman is a powerful, beautiful, fun, world-changing thing. I'm striving to live my life with authority and creativity and authenticity, and I hope to help you do the same.

I love you. I'm in your corner, always.

And now, Carl.

First of all, a major round of applause for Carl Wilson for

designing the world's most beautiful book cover. You make everything better and more beautiful, and this book is no exception.

The second thing I want to recognize is the fact that when your partner chooses to take on a gigantic project like writing a book, you're taking it on too. You're there for the ups and the downs, there to wipe tears and to say, "Get up, you have to keep going." You're there to do a thousand brainstorming sessions. For you, in particular, you were there for a thousand iterations of titles, subtitles, and book cover concepts, and that doesn't even get into all the times you took more onto your mental load and your to-do list because I was working on this.

I'm so grateful.

More than that, I'm grateful for your help. This is your book too. This book came out of a thousand conversations we've had along the way about life and the world and history and culture. Thank you for writing this story with me. Thank you for living this story with me. More than anyone else in my life, you have reminded me that I get to decide, that we get to decide. You are my great love, my best friend, and the best partner in everything. I love the life we're creating together, and I love you.

And last, but certainly not least, to you, my reader. I've had the honor and privilege of leading our online community of women for more than ten years now, and I truly can't believe this is my full-time job. I love this work, and I love y'all. I think you're amazing. I'm in your corner, and I cannot wait to see what you do next.

A SPECIAL THANK-YOU

There's an extra special group of women who were the very first to cheer me on as I was sharing this book with the world. Thank you for being such an integral part of bringing this book to life! I'm so grateful for each and every one of you:

Abby Gohde, Abigail (Stecker) Ernest, Adriana Shaw,
AJ Timberlake, Alaina Goodwin, Alana Cooper, Alex Seward,
Alexa Hahs, Alexandra W., Ally Buckallew, Ally Bumgardner,
Ally Maurer, Alyssa Dieken, Amanda B. Lavallee,
Amanda Gail Smith, Amanda Latham, Amy Howe, Amy O'Leary,
Amy Washburn, Angela Rose Adkins, Anna Bernin-Mallin,
Anna Brown, Anna Fata Shemin, Anna Mamalat, Anna Pollard,
Anna Trotsenko, Anne Littlepage, Anne Matthews, Anne Skovbo,
Annette Lofing, Annie Dupee, Arrielle Jones, Ashley B.,
Ashley Bigos, Ashley Dyer, Ashley Fiegel, Ashley Lonsbury,
Ashley Osborne, Ashley Stafford, Ashley Todd, Ashley Wengerd,
Ashley Whitehead, Ashtynn Robillard, Audrey Pickering,
Autumn Bogucki, Autumn Heath, Bailey Blair, Bailey Seay,
Bec Stewart, Beth Cantu, Bethany A. Beeghley, Bethany Haynie,
Betsabé Pulido Casla, Bre'Ana Davis, Briana Rose,
Brianna McMillion, Bridgette Campbell, Brittany Sabedra,
Brittney Robinson, Brytton Bennett, Caitlin Milam,
Caitlin Sewell, Carissa Joy Strum, Carla Simmons,

Carly Guion, Carol Weston, Caroline Ayers, Caroline Nunez,
Carrie Ferrando, Casey Drennan, Catie Cangemi, Celeste Rollins,
Chaney Flahive, Chantell Rice, Charlotte Fout, Charlotte Yutzy,
Chelsea Heath, Chelsey Nadeau, Cheryl Ridgaway,
Christen Lee, Christy & Hiyla Carey, Christy Atkinson,
Christy Zbylut, CJ Armstrong, Claire Jacobson,
Clarissa Adamyk Harris has, Claudia Reyes, Colleen McInerney,
Colleen Ritchie, Cora Vasseur, Coral Wood, Corianne Maas,
Courtney Fanning, Courtney Hayden, Courtney Leo,
Cynthia Rösch, Danae Roberge, Danielle Landau, Danielle West,
Darcy Warden, Darnesha Moore, Denali J. Lathrop,
Dominique Kennerly, Douachong Yang, Elena Watson,
Elibel Case, Eliza, Elizabeth Adams, Elizabeth Brenneman,
Elizabeth Bryan, Elizabeth Elliott, Elizabeth Mabe,
Elizabeth Peden, Elizabeth Ritter, Elizabeth White, Emily Carter,
Emily D. Barnes, Emily Duckworth, Emily Joy Long,
Emily Keyser, Emily Leugers, Emily Miels, Emily Petersen,
Emily Tuttle, Emily Weitzel, Emma Stuck, Emmie & Kona Hetu,
Erin Czernicki, Erin Kennedy, Erin Walker (*Beauty*),
Erin Williams, Eva Franz, Felisha Brody, Germine Alfonse,
Gina Guillaume, Grace Sellers, Grace Tervin McElmury,
Grayson Baird, Hailey D., Hailey Reneau, Haley Marie,
Haley Pachelo, Haley Powell, Haley Richter, Hanna Bettag,
Hannah Calvert, Hannah Ehle, Hannah Hicks,
Hannah Jackson, Hannah Nester, Hannah Riley,
Hannah Sanchez, Hayley Gatchell, Heather Caudill,
Heather Jackson, Heather Sweeney, Hennessy Wagner,
Hilary Dozier, Hillary Marker, Hope Atchison, Hope Evans,
Hope Jarrett, Lia Trujillo, India Williams, Irina Wibe,
Isabel Naomi, Jackie Champion, Jaclyn Worley, Jami Lankin,
Jamie Burns, Jamine Coleman, Jana Musselwhite,

Janae Klavano, Janelly Valdez, Jasmin Newton,
Jenaya Newhouse, Jenn VanNostrand, Jenna Patterson,
Jenna Wolthuis, Jenni Cyphers, Jennifer Lyons, Jennifer Saliba,
Jennifer Weiberg, Jenny Bianchini, Jessica Gill,
Jillaine Singleton, Jillian Owens, Jocelyn Walters,
Joelle Wisnieski, Johanna Grum, Jordan Cox, Josette A. Martin,
Julia Flanagan, Julianne Adams, Julie Escobar, Kaaren Hatlen,
Kaela Childers, Kaitlin Sanders, Kaitlyn Johnson,
Kallie Michaelson, Karen Overman, Karen Postupac,
KarenYSLau, Karla Geigel, Kasey Mills, Kat Lau,
Katarina MacFadden, Katelyn Armatys, Katelyn Burkholder,
Katherine Mattingly, Kathryn Wurst, Katie Burke, Katie Duncan,
Katie Fails, Katie Gandari, Katie Ochoa, Katie Storm,
Katie Walker, Kayla Hintz, Kayla Johnson, Kayla McMillen,
Kayla Risher, Kelley Puga, Kelsea Gale Beville, Kelsey Antrim,
Kelsey Diane Barber, Kelsey Lehman, Kelsey Phillips,
Kelsie Wood, Kendall Mills, Kendra S. Stevenson, Keri Schnaidt,
Kim Ouwerkerk, Kimberly Clawson, Kimberly Hidalgo Hernandez,
Kinsey Poff, Klaire Mathews, Krista Johnson, Kristen Conway,
Kristen Lomen, Kristen Powell, Kristen Shealy, Kristen Young,
Kristin Gleason, Kristin Jdiener, Kristin Marie, Kristin Theilen,
Kristin Zink, Kristina Figueroa, Kristina Finney, Krystal Gwynn,
Kylie Allison, Kylie Gaeth, Laramie Kettler, Laura Beckert,
Laura Godwin, Laura Heemer, Laura Perticara, Laura Quam,
Laura Thrasher, Laura Williams, Laurel Meyer,
Lauren Ashley Theis, Lauren Auten, Lauren Chang,
Lauren Ralph, Lauren Zook, Leah Hughes, Lesli Lair,
Leslie Bender, Leslie Diaz, Lia Trujillo, Lilybeth Reyes,
Lindsay Jones, Lindy Reynolds, Lise Skovbo, Liz Lesniak,
Lizzie Webster, Luca Katherine Slaughter, Lydia Drabik,
Lyndsie Harris, Mackenzie Dills, Madison Caputi,

Madison Hickman, Madison Willson, Maggie Parrott,
Mallory Hanson, Mallory Latimer, Mallory Whitman,
Mardi Butler, Mariah Gibbons, Marie Benzschawel, Mary Cowan,
Mary McGeeney, Mary-Teresa Lee, Megan Barrett,
Megan Curry, Megan Hovell, Megan Schneickert, Megan Smith,
Megan Souter, Meghan Allen, Meghan McCrann,
Melanie Clawson, Melissa A. Rainwater, Mélissa Drolet,
Michaela Satterfield Roberts, Michaela Ste. Marie,
Michele Phelps, Michelle Bosman, Michelle Brytowski,
Michelle Cooper, Michelle Gresser, Michelle Hartwig,
Michelle Naczi, Michelle Spencer, Mikaila Hudson, Mikey Kim,
Miranda Lord, Miranda Maples, Missy Shouse, Molly Southern,
Molly Taylor, Monica G. Sanchez, Morgan Pierce,
Morgan Shepherd, Mrs. Jordan L. Baker, Nasia Hernandez,
Natalia Sledge, Natalie Browning, Natalie Merrill,
Natalie Sensenig, Nicole Cloyd, Nicole Goza, Nicole Kennedy,
Nina Furnari, Olivia C., Olivia Wallace, Paige Deur,
Pam Hickinbotham, Quincy Livchak, Rachael Dague,
Rachael Naeger, Rachel Edwards, Rachel Faye Jones,
Rachel Lohman, Rachel McDonald, Rachel R. Saylor,
Rachel Wilson, Randi Backscheider, Raquel Velasquez,
Rebecca Bolshaw, Rebecca Leland, Rebecca Lum,
Rebecca Voogt, Rebekah Crawford, Rebekah Moore,
Rebekah Slabach, Rebekah Webb, Rita Marie Doll,
Sabrina Langner, Sam Jenkins, Samantha DeSpirito,
Samantha Kate Herrmann, Samantha Lang, Samantha Thomas,
Sammie Gibbs, Sara Barton, Sara I. Wells, Sara Meshreky,
Sarah B. Guerrier, Sarah Basco, Sarah Easley, Sarah Fox,
Sarah Grube, Sarah Hubbard, Sarah Huntley, Sarah Lise Pierre,
Sarah Scherrer, Sarah Starnes, Shannon Denien, Shannon Etz,
Shannon Martin, Shannon Stearman, Shelby Young McDaniel,

A SPECIAL THANK-YOU

Sheridan Tennant, Sierra Macfarlane, Stacey Yokley,
Stefanie Partin, Stephanie 'Stevie' Taylor, Stephanie Fiorenza,
Stephanie Khumalo, Stephanie Mora, Summer Faith Causey,
Suzannah Waddington, Sydney Markle, Tana Turner,
Terry Lee Crandall, Tiffani McCormick, Tiffany Chichester,
Tiffany Kral, Tory Reinheimer, Tricia Tauer, Trinity Leland,
Vera Ulrich, Victoria Provost, Victoria Sawyer

NOTES

Chapter Two: This Is Not All in Your Head

1. Meg Jay, *The Defining Decade* (New York: Twelve, 2012).
2. "The Teen Brain: 7 Things to Know," National Institute of Mental Health, accessed December 5, 2023, https://www.nimh .nih.gov/health/publications/the-teen-brain-7-things-to-know.
3. Meg Jay, *The Defining Decade*.
4. Jeffrey Jensen Arnett, "Emerging Adulthood: A Theory of Development from the Late Teens through the Twenties," *American Psychologist*, May 2000, https://jeffreyarnett.com /ARNETT_Emerging_Adulthood_theory.pdf.
5. "Jack Needs Jill to Get Up the Hill," *Virginia Magazine*, Fall 2009, https://uvamagazine.org/articles/jack_needs_jill_to_get _up_the_hill.
6. Jane Kelly, "'Shocking' New Research Finds Friendships Are Key to Good Health," *UVA Today*, May 26, 2017, https://news .virginia.edu/content/shocking-new-research-finds-friendships -are-key-good-health.
7. Luisa Dillner, "Is Having No Social Life as Bad for You as Smoking?," *The Guardian*, January 11, 2016, https://www .theguardian.com/lifeandstyle/2016/jan/11/is-having-no -social-life-as-bad-for-you-as-smoking; Zara Abrams, "The Science of Why Friendships Keep Us Healthy," *Monitor on Psychology* 54, no. 4 (June 2023), https://www.apa.org/monitor /2023/06/cover-story-science-friendship.

Chapter Three: It's a Long Story

1. Kate Nicholson, "The 'Woman Question,'" UNC History Department, accessed December 20, 2023, https://hist259.web .unc.edu/thewomanquestion/; Wikipedia, s.v. "The Woman Question," last modified November 26, 2023, 15:23, https://en .wikipedia.org/wiki/The_woman_question.

2. Barbara Ehrenreich and Deirdre English, *For Her Own Good: Two Centuries of the Experts' Advice to Women* (New York: Anchor Books, 2005).

3. Erica Sandberg, "The History of Women and Credit Cards," Bankrate, March 1, 2023, https://www.bankrate.com/finance /credit-cards/history-of-women-and-credit-cards/.

4. Barbara Ehrenreich and Deirdre English, *For Her Own Good*.

5. Raymon Huston, ed., and R. Adam Dastrup, *People, Places, and Cultures*, https://open.library.okstate.edu/culturalgeography /chapter/7-1/.

6. "The Cult of Domesticity," America in Class, National Humanities Center, accessed December 20, 2023, https:// americainclass.org/the-cult-of-domesticity/; Wikipedia, s.v. "Culture of Domesticity," last modified December 14, 2023, 17:28, https://en.wikipedia.org/wiki/Culture_of_Domesticity.

7. Elinor Evans, "From Family to Factory: Women's Lives During the Industrial Revolution," History Extra, March 14, 2022, https://www.historyextra.com/period/industrial-revolution /womens-lifes-roles-industrial-revolution/.

8. "Women in World War II," The National WWII Museum, accessed December 20, 2023, https://www .nationalww2museum.org/students-teachers/student -resources/research-starters/research-starters-women-world -war-ii.

9. "Pink Collar Jobs," Academy to Innovate HR, accessed December 20, 2023, https://www.aihr.com/hr-glossary/pink -collar-jobs/.

10. Katherine Haan, "Gender Pay Gap Statistics in 2023," *Forbes*, February 27, 2023, https://www.forbes.com/advisor/business /gender-pay-gap-statistics/.

Chapter Four: Building the Plane

1. Becky Little, "See How Women Traveled in 1920," *National Geographic*, August 24, 2018, https://www.nationalgeographic .com/travel/article/women-equality-day-history-politics -passport.
2. Audiey Kao, "History of Oral Contraception," *AMA Journal of Ethics*, June 2000, https://journalofethics.ama-assn.org/article /history-oral-contraception/2000-06.
3. "Median Age at First Marriage: 1890 to Present," U.S. Census Bureau, accessed December 20, 2023, https://www.census.gov /content/dam/Census/library/visualizations/time-series/demo /families-and-households/ms-2.pdf.
4. April Yanyuan Wu, Nadia S. Karamcheva, Alicia H. Munnell, and Patrick J. Purcell, "How Do Trends in Women's Labor Force Activity and Marriage Patterns Affect Social Security Replacement Rates?," *Social Security Bulletin* 73, no. 4 (2013), https://www.ssa.gov/policy/docs/ssb/v73n4/v73n4p1.html.
5. Janet L. Yellen, "The History of Women's Work and Wages and How It Has Created Success for Us All," The Brookings Institution, May 2020, https://www.brookings.edu/articles/the -history-of-womens-work-and-wages-and-how-it-has-created -success-for-us-all/.
6. "Why Do We Have a Harder Time Choosing When We Have More Options?," The Decision Lab, accessed December 20, 2023, https://thedecisionlab.com/biases/choice-overload-bias.

Chapter Five: You Get to Decide

1. "Vocation," Frederick Buechner official website, accessed December 20, 2023, https://www.frederickbuechner.com/quote-of-the-day/2017/7/18/vocation.

Chapter Eight: Get Inspired

1. "The Cabinet," The White House official website, accessed December 5, 2023, https://www.whitehouse.gov/administration/cabinet/.

Chapter Nine: Get Moving

1. Jaison R. Abel and Richard Deitz, "Agglomeration and Job Matching among College Graduates," *Federal Reserve Bank of New York Staff Reports*, no. 587 (December 2012; revised December 2014), https://www.newyorkfed.org/medialibrary/media/research/staff_reports/sr587.pdf.
2. Marie Kondo, *The Life-Changing Magic of Tidying Up: The Japanese Art of Decluttering and Organizing* (New York: Ten Speed Press, 2014).

Chapter Ten: What If Your People Disagree?

1. Amy Poehler, *Yes Please* (New York: Dey Street, 2014).

Welcome to Girls Night: The go-to podcast for women in their Everything Era!

8 million downloads & counting!

Navigating big decisions & life transitions one girls night at a time!

The best girls nights aren't just about eating pizza in sweatpants with your friends. They're about problem solving and leaning into the collective wisdom of women, and that's what this podcast is all about.

Join host Stephanie May Wilson as she interviews some of the world's wisest known women on the topics that keep us up at night. You'll walk away from each episode with both clarity and confidence–knowing what your next step is and how to take it.

You don't have to do this alone. We saved a seat just for you!

To tune in, scan the QR code or visit
StephanieMayWilson.com/Listen